Consumer's Guide to
Buying & Selling Gold,
Silver and Diamonds

Consumer's Guide to Buying & Selling Gold, Silver and Diamonds

by I. Jack Brod with Tad Tuleja

Doubleday & Company, Inc., Garden City, New York,

Library of Congress Cataloging in Publication Data

Brod, I. Jack.
    Consumer's guide to buying & selling gold, silver, and diamonds.

    Bibliography: p. 191
    Includes index.
    1. Gold.   2. Silver.   3. Diamonds.   I. Tuleja, Tad, 1944–   .   II. Title.
HQ289.B76   1985   332.63   84–5918
ISBN 0-385-27848-9

Numismatic Coin Grades
From 1983 Handbook of US Coins
© 1983 by Western Publishing Company, Inc.
Reprinted by permission.

CONTENTS

INTRODUCTION

THE $300 "BARGAIN" RING

About a year ago, a well-dressed, soft-spoken young man came into my office at the Empire Gold Buying Service and handed me a ring. It was a simple but attractive engagement ring, with a thin gold band and a one-eighth-carat diamond in a rather heavy-pronged setting. I assumed he had bought it for his sweetheart, and complimented him on his choice.

"I need to sell it," he said. "How much do you think it's worth?"

A little taken aback at his abruptness, I took out my jeweler's eyepiece and began to examine the ring more closely. Through the glass I could see that, while the stone had been neatly cut, it was quite a run-of-the-mill diamond. The color was slightly yellow, and with my ten-power magnifier I could see a small black crystal below the face; from experience I knew it was safe to assume that the heavy-pronged setting concealed even larger flaws. The gold band was 14-karat—again, nothing out of the ordinary.

Feeling sorry about what I thought was the young man's misfortune in love, I took out the eyepiece and handed the ring back to him. I hoped he had not paid more than a hundred dollars or so for it, for I knew that no buyer would give him more than half of that in return.

"It's worth about fifty dollars," I said.

He looked as if all the gold in Fort Knox had just fallen on his foot.

"Fifty dollars!" he cried. "Why, I bought this ring as an investment almost three years ago. That's even less than I paid for it then."

"How much did you pay for it?" I asked.

"Three hundred dollars," he said glumly.

"Well," I told him as gently as I could, "if you hold on to it for another fifteen or twenty years, it could be worth that much. Right now I'm afraid the best price you could get would be fifty dollars. Most jewelers would offer you less."

"But I don't understand this," he wailed. "The man who sold me the ring said it was a real bargain. He said that the price of gold was skyrocketing, and that diamonds were always a good investment. He was sure that if I kept the ring for a few years, it would double or triple in value. I was going to keep it longer, but I needed the money now."

At least, I thought to myself, I had been wrong about the sweetheart. That was a comfort to me, though it could not have been much of one to this would-be jewelry tycoon.

"Look," I explained to him. "This is a very nice ring. The stone is well cut, the setting is nicely done, and as an adornment—as a gift or as an item of beauty—it's a lovely thing to have. But as an investment it's useless. You bought it about three years ago? At that time the gold in the band would have been worth about ten or twelve dollars, the diamond about another thirty-five. The raw materials, in other words, should have fetched forty-five or fifty dollars then. They're worth a little more today, but not in a buyer's market, which is where you're trying to sell it. I'm sorry, but that's the way it is."

"Are you telling me," he asked, "that this is not a real diamond? I mean, is it some kind of fake?"

"It's a real diamond, all right. It's just not worth what you paid for it."

He shook his head in dismay and looked at the stone. "So I guess I'm stuck with it. I can't even bring it back to the guy who sold it to me. They just went out of business."

That figures, I thought to myself. We shook hands, and the young man left.

My first reaction, after he had gone, was anger. In the fifty years I have been in the business of buying and selling precious stones and metals, I had heard a thousand tales like his, and I had never gotten used to it: each new one made me angry.

For I knew exactly what had happened. The reason it didn't surprise me to learn that the seller of the ring had gone out of business was that, in the jewelry trade, fly-by-night operations are legion—and getting more so all the time. I knew just what kind of a joint it was where he had purchased his "bargain" investment. It was a storefront business just off a main thoroughfare, with a big, flashy sign advertising "top prices" for diamonds and gold, and it was run by a smooth-talking individual who, a year before or a week before, had been selling paint or men's suits or snowshoes.

The young man had gone into this place in good faith, rashly told the smooth talker how much he had to spend, and the guy had said to himself, "OK, this kid has got three long ones to drop; I'll stick him with the one-eighth-carat."

The gold and diamond "expert" had probably purchased the ring for thirty or forty dollars a couple of months before, had the diamond reset so its more obvious flaws would be hidden, and unloaded it on the unsuspecting young man at a huge markup. Thinking about it made me mad all over again.

My second reaction was calmer. If only the young man had come to me first, I thought, I could have saved him a lot of trouble. If he had showed me the ring *before* buying it, I could have told him exactly what it was worth, and he might have saved his money.

I thought about that for a while. I thought about all the little things you pick up in fifty years in the business, and about how I could have mentioned just a few of them to him and saved him three hundred dollars.

I could have told him, for example, that not all gold is alike: that the gold which is used to make jewelry is generally 14- or 18-karat gold, and that this grade of gold is not worth anywhere near the "market price" of 24-karat, or pure, gold. He probably had been told that his gold ring would be worth, per ounce, whatever the London price fixers said that "gold" was worth on a given day. In fact it would always be worth only a little over half of that. I could have told him that there was nothing *wrong* with 14-karat gold—unless you paid a 24-karat price for it.

I could have told him that diamonds are not necessarily a boy's best friend. I could have pointed out that these stones come in a wide range of colors, cuts and clarity—so that a one-carat stone, for example, might be worth anything from $500 to $30,000, depending on a variety of factors. He was apparently under the impression that a diamond was a diamond was a diamond. I was sure that the man who sold him the stone had not bothered to mention its yellow color or its obvious flaw.

I could have told him how, in the jewelry business, the retail value of an item is generally the result of a 400 percent markup over the actual metal and stone value. Jewelers don't work for nothing, and neither do goldsmiths and stone setters; the young man had evidently not been aware that middleman charges had been added to the supposed "market" value of his "investment." Buying such a ring as an investment, I could have told him, was like buying a woolen blanket in the hope that fleece would skyrocket in value.

I thought about all this for a while, and then I made a decision.

If I hadn't been able to help that one disappointed young man, maybe I could help others who might just as easily get cheated in today's razzle-dazzle gold and diamond markets. Maybe I could put down on paper some of the things I had learned in my fifty years in the business, so that prospective stone and metal buyers—speculators as well as "investors"—might be spared the grief of learning, as he had, that they might have to wait twenty years or longer before their purchase earned back its price.

And so this book was born.

Buying gold, silver, diamonds and precious stones has become an extremely popular hedge against inflation in the past decade, and it has brought some people security. But for every person who successfully negotiates the perils of the precious stone and metal markets, there are dozens of people who have lost money through a combination of ignorance, eagerness and the cleverness of disreputable dealers.

That is why it is crucial for the prospective buyer to be aware of the tricks of the trade (and I do mean tricks) before he or she enters into negotiation for that once-in-a-lifetime "bargain." I hope this book will serve that purpose.

You would be amazed at some of the things that go on in the gold and jewelry business. I have seen rings bought in the morning and sold the same afternoon for five times the original price. I have seen "genuine" Burmese rubies that came in fact from Thailand—and were worth, therefore, a fraction of what an innocent buyer might pay for them. I have seen diamonds that should have been cut to three quarters of a carat actually cut to a full carat, because the larger (though inferior-cut) stone would bring a higher price from the unaware. In recent years, I have seen stones so skillfully painted (painting, or "coating," is a time-honored ruse in the diamond trade) that even a high-powered microscope could not detect the fraud.

And these are only the outright, clearly illegal aspects of the trade. There are also plenty of suspicious but perfectly legal "tricks" which lie in wait for the uninformed: like the jeweler's tactic of getting you, the prospective seller of a ring, to tell *him* what you want for it. Supposedly reputable dealers use this ploy all the time, because they know that in many cases your asking price will be ludicrously low.

If you're one of the thousands of Americans who are appalled to see your savings being eaten up by inflation; if you have a little money to invest but not enough for blue-chip stocks or a money-market fund; if you have heard about the "great killings" to be made in the precious-metal and diamond markets and yet are wary of getting stung—then this book may be the guide you are looking for.

It is possible to invest sensibly in precious stones and metals, but you have to approach the task judiciously, and you have to know the pitfalls. Like any other investment field, the gold and diamond field can be risky, because although there are thousands of reputable dealers across the country, there are also a fair number of crooks. Not everybody with a ten-power loupe and a stone to test gold is a trustworthy person to deal with, and before you invest in precious metals or stones, you should be able to tell the good guys from the bad.

Plenty of people cannot. Hundreds of would-be investors are wiped out completely each year by such common frauds as the street-corner hustler peddling "hot" gold chains which are stamped "14 K" but made of brass. Thousands more are fleeced by "bucket shop" operators selling phony metals certificates; these operators—who choose their unfortunate clients from lists of doctors, executives and Cadillac owners—routinely garner millions of dollars before the authorities can pin them down. In spite of government regulation, and in spite of the jewelry industry's own strict guidelines, such schemes are far from uncommon. If you get stung by one of them, it won't matter much to you that the majority of dealers are honest.

What I hope this book will do is to give you a broad picture of the fascinating world of buying and selling gold, silver and diamonds, and then show you how to move about in that world without ending up penniless. I'll be talking about market prices and appraisals, bullion and medallions and coins, grading procedures and flaws, and common con games and how you can guard against them. Keep in mind that, given the fluctuations of the market, there is no way to keep the prices quoted throughout the book current; you'll need to check on today's prices. When you've finished the book, you should realize that, even if you have only a few hundred dollars to spend, you can still make wise investments. And I hope you will see that, if it is played with care, the precious stone and metal "game" can bring you enjoyment as well as profit.

The young man who came to me with his "bargain" had made a mistake based mainly on ignorance. In my fifty years in this business, I have made my share of mistakes too—and learned a lot from them. That is why I think you can profit from this book.

Perhaps, somewhere out there, that young man will too.

PART I

THE MAGIC METAL

CHAPTER 1

THE EL DORADO FACTOR

In the century that followed Columbus' discovery of the New World, the jungles of what is now Colombia were the site of one of the strangest adventures ever to occupy the European mind.

There, amid the snakes and mosquitoes and fever, Spanish soldiers of fortune pursued a dream that would bring them, they were convinced, lives of luxury and ease. Under such leaders as Jiménez de Quesada, Gonzalo Pizarro, and Lope de Aguirre, they trekked doggedly, circuitously through the headwaters of the Amazon so that, at the end of their journeys, they could gaze on El Dorado.

The belief in El Dorado, the continent's hidden city of gold, had its origins in an Indian legend. According to the traditions of the Chibcha tribe, a golden god had dropped from the sky in ancient times and descended into the dark waters of a mountain lake. Once a year, the Chibcha sent one of their chiefs into this lake to memorialize the god's visit. Anointing him first with balsam gum, they would spray him with powdered gold, which, when he dove into the lake, would be washed off as an offering to the god. The bottom of the lake, they said, was a field of gold.

According to most accounts, the last performance of this ritual took place around 1480, a good decade before Columbus landed in the Caribbean. But tales of the ceremony persisted, and by the time Quesada first saw the Colombian wilderness, in the 1530s, the story of El Dorado—Spanish for "the Gilded One"—had been transformed from a local tradition into the germ of a fabulous legend.

To Quesada's soldiers, El Dorado was not the protagonist in a Chibcha religious ceremony but the image of all worldly dreams. El Dorado, they began to believe, was not a man but a place: a city of such unbelievable splendor that anyone who found it in the jungle would find himself richer than a king. No wonder they followed their leader through such hell. At a time when European princes weighed the wealth of their kingdoms almost exclusively in gold, such quixotic forays into the jungle were not at all uncommon.

But quixotic they certainly were. In all of Quesada's wanderings, in all the wanderings of those who came in his wake, no solid evidence was uncovered that El Dorado in fact existed. The city, like the dream, was a phantom: for over a hundred years, Europe searched for a ghost. In the process, scores of adventurers perished; no more than a handful got rich.

From the perspective of the modern world, it is easy to see the quest for El Dorado as a mere historical delusion—a mania whose social history belongs with the history of witches and dragons. But that is more facile than accurate. We moderns may have escaped our ancestors' grosser social fantasies, but our fascination with gold is not fundamentally very different from that which drove men toward El Dorado. There is a mysterious, almost magical appeal to gold that is as much a factor in its value today as it was four centuries ago.

People who are unfamiliar with how gold is traded tend to overlook this fact and to assume that the high price of the metal is a result of its inherent usefulness or rarity. Actually, the utility and rarity of gold have relatively little to do with its price. That price, far more than the price of other commodities, comes about because human beings attach a special reverence to the metal. Judged purely on the basis of utility and rarity, gold is incredibly overpriced.

Perhaps this sounds heretical to you—especially coming from someone who has spent a lifetime dealing in gold. But I assure you it is quite true. What's more, it has always been true. Gold, because of its allure, has always been somewhat overpriced. The Spaniards of the sixteenth century did not approach the sheer folly of today's inflated pricing, but they did set a value on gold far in excess of its "utility" value.

If you doubt that, consider Quesada in the wilderness. Finding himself surrounded by some of the richest natural resources on earth, he chose to hunt for El Dorado. To a shipbuilding nation like Spain, the Americas' vast timber stores would have been a far more "useful" resource than the metal. What did he see in gold?

The same question might be asked today. Gold is a rare metal, yes, and its uses have increased considerably since Quesada's day. But neither the uses nor the relative scarcity of gold has increased so much that it warrants $400 an ounce on the market. If rarity and utility were the only criteria of price, we would expect other metals (such as platinum or iridium) to be priced way above gold.

Gold does have more than symbolic value. For example, its malleability makes it useful in jewelry (just as it was useful in the sixteenth century) and also in dental work (something that Quesada did not much concern himself with). It is a good conductor of heat and electricity, which makes it valuable in electronics. It can be beaten or stretched to an almost infinite thinness, and because of this it is used as a coating —to provide heat shields, for example, for space visors. And it is quite pretty. Its color was admired long before it was thought to be valuable as money, and the fact that it does not tarnish only increases its aesthetic appeal.

Yet these uses do not account for the worldwide price of gold. That price continues to be high for very much the same reason it was high in Quesada's day: because the metal was *thought of* as valuable.

Its value, in other words, is a psychological convention. Gold is important because it has *always* been important. The recent surge in its price is not connected, in a significant way, to jewelry or electronics, and if its usefulness declined—if, for example, a cheap substitute could be found for gold fillings—there is little chance that its price would follow suit.

The price of gold, in short, is determined less by utilitarian, economic factors than by how people react to it *emotionally*.

But not just any people. The people whose emotions affect the price of gold are a select and curious lot, and the way they operate says a lot about just how idiosyncratic, just how conventional, the current gold market is.

Let's look a little more closely at these "goldbugs."

THE GOLDBUGS

Nothing so clearly suggests the archaic, romanticized nature of the gold-trading world than the manner in which the daily price of the metal is determined.

With most commodities, of course, price is dependent on all the supply and demand factors at the opening of a given market day. When the market opens, hundreds of brokers vie for the attention of sellers and buyers, and within minutes of the initial commotion, it is clear from the stock-listing board that wheat, or soybeans, or banana oil, is now going up, or down, or remaining steady. With virtually all commodities, it is the interaction of many bidders that sets the daily price for the commodity.

The price of gold, on the other hand, is set by a mere five men.

They are influential men. They live and work in London, the center of world gold trading, and for the past six and a half decades (since 1919), they have been directly responsible for doing for gold what all those shouting bidders do for soybeans.

The five are the heads (or their representatives) of London's five major gold-banking firms: Mocatta and Goldsmid; Sharps, Pixley & Co.; N. M. Rothschild & Sons; Johnson Mathey & Co.; and Samuel Montagu & Co. Each day at precisely 10:30 A.M., the spokesmen for these five firms meet in the Rothschild offices, sit down around a large table, and decide how much you will be able to get on that heirloom ring you are trying to sell. The price they come up with, after negotiation, is known as the London daily "fix," and with a few modifications, it remains the basic working price for gold trading throughout the world on that day.

The modifications are interesting. Firstly, since 10:30 A.M. London time is the middle of the night in the United States, the English gold fixers meet again in the afternoon (at 3 P.M.) to issue a revised price that will be in effect when New York offices open. Secondly, there are price fixes made in Zürich, Switzerland, as well, since so much continental trading goes on there. And thirdly, certain American firms, such as Engelhard and Handy & Harman, set their own prices too. The London price, however, is the base rate for the others, and it is the one you will generally see in newspaper listings when you check the daily rate for gold.

It's an old-fashioned, conventional system, one that has not changed substantially in over sixty years. That in itself says something about the rapidity with which the gold market responds to modern, practical realities.

But Rothschild's is the center of gold fixing not simply because of tradition. Gold traders may be conventional, but they are not backward, and there is a good reason that London remains the center of the gold market. It is because, in spite of the recent influx of American buyers and sellers, the five firms mentioned still control a substantial portion of the world market, both because their clients are very active traders and because of London's traditional relation with South Africa, where the bulk of the world's gold is mined: the British capital remains the brokerage point for all South African gold.

Nor, of course, do these major five goldbugs decide on the gold price entirely alone. They fix the price not on a whim, but in response to their clients' bids at the time the price is to be set. They are less actors than reactors in the drama. It is their job to read the market on any given morning and issue the good news (or bad) to the world. They are, in this sense, like auctioneers who set a reserve price or a price at which bidding can begin. The people who *really* set the gold price—those shadowy goldbugs behind the scenes—are the speculators and major investors, in response to whom the gentlemen at Rothschild's do their negotiation.

Why was it necessary to establish this curious, regimented system for determining the price of gold? Why couldn't gold be allowed to seek its own value in a free-for-all trading market, just as other commodities do? Why did the gold price have to be so centralized, so carefully controlled?

Those questions may be partly beside the point today, because in the past decade gold has been traded rather freely, in the United States as well as abroad. But this has not always been the case, and in order to understand why it was not always the case, you have to know something about gold's peculiar relationship to the international money supply. It is because gold has for so long been a standard for international exchange that it remains so closely regulated. It is because of that, too, that it has always been unique among commodities.

THE UNIQUE COMMODITY

As a commodity, gold is in a class by itself. It follows the laws of supply and demand, but only up to a point: past that point, speculative fevers—the modern version of the El Dorado dream—take over, and they can run the price up astronomically in a short period of time (such as happened in the late 1970s) or cut it in half in just as short a time (such as happened in 1981).

It's a good thing for the commodity market that this fever is peculiar to goldbugs. Dealers in other commodities simply do not have to contend with the enormous shifts in value that have frequently plagued the gold market. The reason for this is simple: The factors that affect the price of soybeans are well known and fairly constant. Government price controls will tend to depress the market, making soybean speculators bearish, while a prolonged drought will cut production and therefore make a price hike likely. People who deal in "soft" commodities such as feed, livestock and crops measure their chances of making money against the known factors of government policy and weather, and can predict with fair reliability in what direction, and how fast, their investments are likely to move. This is not so with gold.

For one thing, even the economic variables that influence the price of gold tend to be far less reliable than weather or even government intervention. Historically, the price of gold has fallen in times of economic stability and risen sharply in times of actual or perceived stress. Domestic or world revolutions, for example, tend to increase hoarding—because when your government is shaky, you become suspicious of currency and start squirreling away money that doesn't float. So political uncertainty can push the gold price way up in a short period of time.

The problem for the investor—especially the small investor—faced with this sort of situation is that, in spite of the "crisis means price hike" rule of thumb, politics is even less predictable than the weather— and this makes gold speculation a lot less easy than speculation with soybeans.

But that's only part of the picture. Added to the inherent restlessness of the gold market in times of political uncertainty is what we might call the El Dorado Factor: that congeries of avarice, wish fulfillment and awe that influences the gold-buying market much more intensely than it does the market for any other commodity. It is this El Dorado Factor, I would suggest, that accounts ultimately for the radical shifts in gold price that we have witnessed in the past decade—and that will continue to be a strong factor in all future price fluctuations.

As a way of looking further at this issue, let's compare the way gold is traded to the way in which another commodity—say wheat—is traded on the international markets.

One of the principal differences between the buying and selling of wheat and the buying and selling of gold is that, within a given time span, most of the wheat that is produced is available for consumption. When it is unavailable, it is because farmers, or governments subsidizing farmers, have withheld or destroyed some wheat in order to raise the price of the rest. In normal circumstances, when ten thousand bushels of wheat are produced, ten thousand bushels can be sold.

Furthermore, if, over the period of a decade, a hundred thousand bushels are produced, it is safe to assume that by the end of the decade, eighty or ninety thousand bushels have long since been consumed. Generally speaking, people do not stockpile commodities.

Except in the case of gold.

Because gold is virtually imperishable, it is extremely easy to hoard. Both private investors and governments have taken frequent advantage of this fact. In fact, *most* of the gold that has been extracted from the earth since gold mining began is not widely circulated, but is kept in huge underground vaults. The bulk of the gold that has been produced has gone into government hoards (the United States has the world's largest) and is still there today. Thus most of the production of this unique commodity does not circulate and is not a major factor in the daily rise and fall in price. This is the fundamental anomaly in gold trading: that the largest owners of the commodity seldom participate in the market.

The reason for this has less to do with the laws of supply and demand than with the more tenuous, often mystical "laws" of international exchange. Gold has long been regarded as a standard of exchange in international trade. It is "bedrock," according to one economist. It is the standard against which all currencies are ultimately measured. And this is no less true today than it was years ago, when the West was still on the "gold standard."

But there are gold standards and gold standards, and in a sense it can be said that we are still on a kind of gold standard: a new gold standard, as opposed to the old gold standard, in which the par value of an ounce of gold was $35. Today, the par values of the dollar and the Mark and the yen have all fallen in relation to gold, and in addition the value of the metal can fluctuate radically up or down because of speculative as well as monetary factors. This is a more complicated situation for gold than was the old gold standard, but it does not mean that gold is not still tremendously important.

To understand this better, let's look at what has happened historically to alter the value of gold in this century.

GOLD STANDARDS: OLD AND NEW

In the "good old days" before the Depression, theoretically every American dollar was backed by a dollar's worth of gold. That was the old gold standard, so beloved of Monopoly players and others who feel gold is still bedrock. That standard, begun in 1900, was never very realistic, considering the growth of modern government, and it lasted only until 1934, when Franklin D. Roosevelt, to rescue a failing economy, temporarily closed the banks, devalued the dollar and announced a new "par" rate between the dollar and gold. Before 1934, the government would pay you about $20 for an ounce of gold; thenceforth, said FDR, the rate would be $35 an ounce.

At the same time, however, under another provision of the Gold Reserve Act, it was determined that private persons could no longer own gold. They could own gold that had been minted *before* the Act went into effect, but nothing minted thereafter. Since this effectively banned speculators from the market, it was hoped it would have a stabilizing effect both on gold and on the dollar. Ten years later, in the famous Bretton Woods agreement, a group of international bankers sought the same stabilizing effect when they established fixed exchange rates for their governments' currencies at a fairly inflexible "par" value and designated the gold : dollar ratio of 1 : 35 as the basic working rate of the whole system.

The Bretton Woods system was in trouble almost as soon as it was established. For the 1 : 35 ratio to operate effectively, people would have to believe that each American dollar was backed by one thirty-fifth of an ounce of gold and that the dollar itself was stable. Within a decade after the end of World War II, it became increasingly obvious that these beliefs were unwarranted. To help the European recovery, the United States sent enormous amounts of money overseas, thus creating a balance-of-payments deficit that was later exacerbated by the dollar drain of the Korean and Vietnam conflicts. The continual outflow of dollars weakened our currency in relation to both gold and other currencies, and the result was the constant threat of a devaluation that would weaken it even further.

President Nixon, alarmed by that threat, tried in 1971 to allay widespread fears that the dollar was turning into a mere paper entity and that our gold supplies—drawn on for years by foreign traders with excess dollars—were severely depleted. As part of his economic policy, he shut the U.S. "gold window," refusing to honor future foreign claims on our gold hoard. And in December of that year he supported what he called "the greatest monetary agreement in the history of the world," the so-called Smithsonian agreement, by which bankers meeting at the Smithsonian Institution, in Washington, D.C., revised the Bretton Woods structure to reflect something closer to reality. The big news of that conference had been awaited for years: the dollar was devalued by 8 percent. A further devaluation of about 10 percent followed two years later.

The Nixon administration hoped that these devaluations would help the U.S. balance of payments by making exports more attractive to foreign customers and imports less attractive here, but that is not exactly what happened. Instead, other governments devalued their currencies to meet the American challenge, and in the end *all* paper currencies became suspect. As Leonard Silk observes in his *Economics in Plain English,* "The fixed exchange rate system could not survive the continuing dollar outflow." The result was a "floating world monetary system," in which the fiction of gold-backed currency was thoroughly exposed and gold was traded freely on the open market. In Silk's rueful phrasing, "The loss of respect for the dollar, the key currency of the world monetary system, brought on a flight from all currencies into anything precious and scarce that would hold its value in a time of monetary crisis—gold, silver, platinum, and many other commodities, all of which seemed suddenly in short supply."

Then, in 1974, the American Government rescinded its 1934 interdiction against private citizens owning gold and agreed to begin selling gold to the public—to "dishoard" some of that enormous stock at Fort Knox, the largest cache of gold in the world. It was expected that this revolutionary move would not only bring in needed cash, but also—by flooding the free market with dishoarded gold—bring down the metal's price and thus (because of the traditional inverse relationship between currencies and gold) improve the dollar.

It was a desperate move, and it didn't work. The rescinding of the ban against private ownership actually only brought in more speculators, and the result was that, half a decade after the market was "liberated," the price of gold had jumped to ten times its 1934 rate. At one point in 1980 it even nudged toward $900 an ounce.

One factor in this huge price hike, according to Timothy Green, may be a kind of "lag effect" by which liberated gold rapidly made up ground it had lost in the years its price was artificially restrained.[1] Remember that throughout the first seventy years of this century, wheat and soybeans and timber all fluctuated in price depending on market factors. Gold did not. It was officially fixed, because it was a standard of international trade, at about $20 an ounce and in 1934 at $35 an ounce. When it was demonetized—when its connection to the dollar was revised—what happened was a quick and extraordinary increase in the metal's attractiveness. That was the lag effect, and it was not in itself surprising.

What is surprising is the rate at which gold has *continued* to rise. The lag effect is hardly enough to account for a price of $850 an ounce, reached in January of 1980—or a drop to half of that within a year. To what can we attribute this madness? To speculators, I am afraid, under the influence of the El Dorado Factor.

But you know much of this already. If you have been reading the papers in the past decade, you already know that gold has jumped, and then fallen, dramatically in the past ten years. What you probably *want* to know is how it will fare in the years ahead—and how you can profit from future fluctuations.

No one can say with certainty how gold will fare in the future. The best a forecaster can do is to give you some idea of how speculators—those prime movers in the battle for the metal's soul—look at the current picture and how they attempt to predict whether we will be in for another hike or a fall in the element's fortunes.

[1] See Green, *How to Buy Gold*.

WHAT THE SPECULATORS LOOK FOR

If the major factor in the price of gold today is what the speculators will pay, it is to your advantage to know what factors they consider in their bidding for the precious metal. There are of course many such factors, but we can isolate six as most prominent. They are 1) supply, 2) demand, 3) currency, 4) crises, 5) dishoarding and 6) interest rates.

1. Supply

We've noted that, in spite of its peculiarities, gold is affected by supply-and-demand factors just like other commodities. Because of that, speculators look first at how much gold is being produced at any given time, how much of it is being made available for international trading, and how much of a demand in the usual fields—jewelry, dentistry and electronics—there is likely to be to feed off this supply.

That sounds simple enough, but there are a couple of other things you have to keep in mind when you talk about supply and demand with gold.

For one thing, the given supply is not "free" in the same way that the supply of wheat or rubber is free. The gold supply is carefully controlled by the governments under whose jurisdictions it is mined. Those governments are the governments of South Africa (which produces about one half the world supply) and the Soviet Union (which accounts for about a quarter).

The amount of South African gold which is made available to the world market is regulated depending on the current market price and the needs of the country's foreign trade. To bolster a poor balance of payments or to reap the benefits of a diminished supply market, the South African Government commonly restricts not only the tonnage of industrial metal released, but also the number of coins, such as the popular Krugerrand, that they mint each year. The Soviet Union does much the same thing, with the added wrinkle that, in response to high gold prices, the Russians frequently expand free-world sales—which tends to depress, and thus regulate, the market.

Between them, these two countries control the availability of about three quarters of currently mined gold. That is nothing compared to international gold reserves, but on a day-to-day basis it is a great deal indeed. It's easy to see that, with 75 percent of the current supply regulated by two governments, the supply factor is a little tricky to determine.

Moreover, throughout the 1970s—whether by government design or by the accidents of mining is difficult to say—the yearly production of gold slowly but steadily fell, from a high of 47,522,000 troy ounces to a low of 39,000,000 troy ounces. This gradual diminution in the available supply has of course tended to push prices upward and has certainly been a factor in the 1970s gold rush.

2. Demand

Generally speaking, as the price of a commodity falls, the amount of the commodity that people will be willing to buy rises: demand is inversely related to price. That rule operates in the gold market, too, and it can be safely said that, as long as the economy is fundamentally sound, the cheaper gold rings or necklaces are, the more of them people will buy. Naturally speculators are sensitive to this aspect of pricing as well.

However, there is a significant difference between gold that is sold for jewelry or dental work and gold that is purchased for speculation or hoarding. Economist Lawrence Rosen has written that the elasticity of demand for luxury products such as gold (that is, the extent to which demand responds to price changes) is usually very high: "a small rise in price will cut purchases substantially, while a modest decline in price will expand the quantity bought by large amounts." This rule, he says, does *not* operate with hoarded gold.

Because hoarded gold is often bought for speculation, it is difficult to determine how demand for it will be affected by the market price. Rosen says that computing the elasticity of demand for hoarding, speculation and investment is next to impossible, since "application of gold to this use is not even remotely measurable by this type of analysis."[2]

3. Currency

Another factor that speculators consider is the reliability of currencies. In spite of the 1971 Smithsonian agreement, gold is still tied to the international exchange system, simply because, whatever the metal's relationship to the dollar, the vast bulk of gold stocks are still in government vaults. There may no longer be a "healthy" connection between the dollar and bullion, but that is not to say that the connection has been severed. The metal in Fort Knox does still provide a theoretical backing for our currency, and because of the worldwide respect paid to gold as a medium of exchange, it is still in great demand. The gold reserves of the suddenly oil-rich countries of the Middle East, for exam-

[2] See Rosen, *When and How to Profit from Buying and Selling Gold.*

ple, have been going up throughout the past decade, as sheikhs who are drowning in petrodollars but are still uneasy about paper currency look to gold as a new foundation of their economies.

Historically, gold and paper currency have been related inversely to each other. When a nation's currency is seen as stable, the price of gold there is low, because people trust the government's money enough not to want to hedge with the hard metal. When a currency is devalued, though, the price of gold goes up, since devaluation makes people nervous and they flock to buy a medium of exchange that can withstand the instabilities of central control.

The speculator has all this in mind as he or she determines when to bid, and how much. If he sees the dollar falling in value, he will probably find gold attractive; if the dollar is stable, the price of gold will go down. We saw this graphically in the years immediately following the government's 1974 opening of the market. The biggest surge to buy gold did not come in 1975, as was expected, but in 1978 and 1979— when the inflation rate was much higher. By 1979, when paper money was seen as relatively worthless, some of my customers had to pay capital-gains taxes on their gold sales—something I had not seen happen since I began buying gold, in 1931.

4. Crises

A fourth, related factor to consider is the stability of the government itself, and by extension the stability of the economy it manages. Harry Browne calls gold a "permanent crisis hedge,"[3] and this is a good phrase to suggest how securely gold has been tied in the past to the fortunes of individual governments. Traditionally, gold has been hoarded to protect against the failure not only of a government's currency, but of the government itself. This is especially true in Europe and the East, and is becoming more so in America.

Wars and rumors of wars—so goes the speculator's adage—are principal ingredients in the rising fortunes of gold. In times of social stability, people don't need to hoard gold. When troops are roaming the streets, the value of the metal skyrockets, because, in a time of upheaval, it is a traditionally accepted medium of exchange. Think, for example, of how many Vietnamese refugees bought their way out of the country with gold after the fall of Saigon, and you will appreciate the honor paid to gold in a crisis.

[3] See Browne, *New Profits from the Monetary Crisis.*

5. Dishoarding

Speculators and investors must be sensitive to a glut of gold on the market. You recall the effect that the United States Government policy of "no private ownership" had on the gold market between 1934 and 1974: it stabilized the price. The opposite effect occurred in the 1970s, when the market was legally opened to speculators. Even though gold is demonetized, private and government dishoarding can still alter the price. Such dishoarding is a major though intermittent factor in the control of the gold price. Lawrence Rosen calls it "the most unpredictable element in forming a strategy about gold prices."[4]

6. Interest Rates

Finally, the level of interest rates affects the price of gold. Unlike an investment in a money-market fund, an investment in gold pays no interest. Therefore, when interest rates are high, fewer investors are interested in gold, and the price falls. When they are low, the money-markets seem less attractive and people seek out gold, thus driving the price up.

These are among the factors that the big-time speculators—the people who move behind Rothschild's—take into account every day as they decide whether to buy or sell. Even if you're considering buying only a few hundred dollars' worth of the metal, it is wise for you to be aware of these factors too.

A PIECE OF EL DORADO

There is, of course, another factor: the one I have called the El Dorado Factor, or the presence in the gold market of emotional and unpredictable decision making. Louis Rukeyser, at the height of the 1980 gold fever, made an indirect reference to this factor when he claimed that "the recent gyrations of the gold market don't require financial analysis so much as psychoanalysis. . . . Hot emotion, rather than cool discernment, determines the daily price of gold."[5] Fear, anxiety, greed, wishful thinking, gamblers' hunches—all these play a part in the fluctuations of this mysterious, long-honored metal. The Londoners who fix the price each day may be sober, pin-striped bankers; many of the speculators are not.

[4] Rosen, op. cit., p. 47.
[5] See Rukeyser, "Gold price equals fear plus greed," in Philadelphia *Bulletin,* Jan. 31, 1980.

Because this is so, you would be well advised to enter the gold market with caution. You may read the daily fixes regularly, you may know just how much gold has been produced in South Africa this year, you may be certain that the gold-chain fad is going to last one more year—and you may still get burned.

That is why I advise you to buy into the gold market only with "risk capital"—that is, with money that you can afford to lose, supposing you guess wrong. This does not mean you should keep away from the game. On the contrary, I have found it to be one of the most fascinating and lucrative ventures around. But you should know, before you begin playing it, that there are real risks involved, even when everything is on the up and up. So be careful with your money, and don't assume that you can play, even with "bedrock," recklessly.

Before you invest, you have to know what to buy. Gold, says Harry Browne, is a kind of insurance policy against hard times.[6] This is a good way to look at it, but of course there's no point in having an insurance policy if what you pay for it is ten times as much as the return you will earn if it has to be cashed in. Your goal as an investor should be not simply to get the biggest policy you can, but to spend your funds intelligently so that what you get serves you well in both sane and insane times. The trick is to purchase your piece of El Dorado without getting mired down, as Jiménez de Quesada's soldiers did, in the jungle.

Not all gold investments can do that for you. Many of them, in fact, can be no better as investments than paper money itself—and some can be a whole lot worse.

If you have a small amount of risk capital and you wish to invest it in gold, the first thing you need to know, therefore, is what *kind* of gold to buy. Which piece of El Dorado do you want? The first step that the small investor such as yourself needs to take is to investigate the options that are open and to weigh the pluses and minuses of each one. The next chapter will explain these options.

---

[6] Browne, op. cit., pp. 210–11.

CHAPTER 2

GOLD: YOUR OPTIONS

Because gold has long been the symbol of success, the standard against which all value is finally measured, many novice goldbugs assume that buying it, in any form and from any seller, is basically a pretty good gamble. Gold is so desirable, they think, that it is worth almost any price. They are like Spain's Charles I, who, dazzled by the very idea of gold, instructed his sixteenth-century soldiers of fortune, "Get it! At all costs, bring me gold!"

Now, while it is true that gold is almost universally appreciated and that it retains its value much better than virtually any other commodity, this definitely does not mean that buying it is a free ride. Trading in the precious metal is like trading in anything else: you should approach your gold transactions not with the mystical enthusiasm of the sixteenth century, but with the hardheaded caution that is advisable in any other transaction.

Say you were going to buy an automobile and that you were financially well enough off to be able to shop for a Cadillac. How would you go about it?

You might, if you were dazzled by the prospect of buying such a prestige item, simply walk into the nearest Cadillac dealer, point to the model you liked, and pull out your checkbook and pen. Or you might be more cautious. You might talk to several dealers, ask about prices, models and options, and check with each dealer on installment payments, service availability, insurance charges, sales taxes and trade-in value. If you were being cautious, you would hold off making a decision until you had carefully weighed the answers to all your questions.

Even if you were the first kind of buyer—the one who simply slaps down his checkbook and asks the salesman, "How much?"—you might still get a pretty good deal. General Motors (its current troubles aside) is an old and respected company, and as long as you purchased the car new from a reliable dealer, you would probably end up satisfied.

But think how much surer you would be of satisfaction if you took the second approach. Think how much more confident you would be that the transaction was sound if you settled your uncertainties in advance, rather than discovering, once you got the car in your garage, that the warranty was for only six months or that your dealer was going out of business.

If everything went as planned, you'd have nothing to worry about no matter which way you bought the car. But if anything went wrong, you would be happier if you had been cautious than if you had been cavalier.

The same thing goes for gold. Gold is the Cadillac of commodities, but just because it is a prestige purchase doesn't mean that all of it is alike, or that one dealer is as good as another. If you have decided to invest in gold, you should begin by shopping around and asking questions. That's the only way you're going to know whether or not you are dealing with someone reliable.

In the following chapter, I'll give you some detailed advice on what to look for in a dealer. Here I want to give you a few of the basic terms you will need to know, with any dealer, when you go shopping for gold. Dealers all use these terms, and it is therefore important for you to understand them before you consider a purchase. Not knowing them when you buy gold is like shopping for a $15,000 car without knowing the difference between an air filter and radial tires: you *can* conclude a transaction that way, but you'll be far better protected with some background.

GOLD BUYING: BASIC TERMS

Just as not all Cadillacs are alike, so, too, not all gold is alike. It is not enough for you to know that what you are buying is "gold"; you need to know, in addition, what *quality* of gold it is and in what *quantity* you are buying (or selling) it.

1. Quality

The quality of gold is measured in terms of *fineness* and of *karats.* Let's talk about fineness first. Perfectly fine, or pure, gold is gold that contains virtually nothing but the element itself. It is, for all practical purposes, 100 percent gold. This quality of gold is obviously the most desirable, but it is also relatively rare. Most of the gold produced today contains not only gold but one or more additional elements known as *alloys,* and when a piece of gold is alloyed with copper or nickel or even silver, it is no longer considered pure, even though the amount of alloy may be very small.

Gold is alloyed with other metals for a variety of reasons. Alloying permits a refiner to stretch the more valuable metal, so that less of it need be used in the final product: obviously this saves him money. In addition, gold is alloyed because, being an extremely soft metal, it is not as practical when it is unalloyed than when it is mixed with a hardening agent; alloying thus increases the durability of the gold product. Alloying is also done simply to alter the metal's appearance: what is commonly known as "white gold," for example, is an alloy of gold and nickel.

There is nothing wrong with alloyed gold, and indeed if it weren't for alloying, most of the world's coinage and virtually all of its golden jewelry would long ago have been worn down to nothing. Completely fine gold is just too soft to be useful as a day-to-day commodity.

As an *investment,* however, pure gold is the top of the line. Since most gold bought as an investment is handled very rarely, refiners can and do make it in an almost 100 percent pure form. If you are buying gold as an investment, therefore, you should always know the *degree of fineness* of your purchase before you put any money down.

Most gold bars and many medallions and coins that are manufactured for investment and speculation today are stamped at the refinery with a number that indicates fineness. This number is one of the things that you will always want to know when you are buying or selling the metal. It is a decimal number expressed in thousandths (sometimes ten-thousandths), and it indicates precisely how much pure gold your bar or medallion contains.

Say you are looking at a gold bar stamped ".9975 fine." What that number tells you is that the bar contains 9,975 parts out of 10,000 pure gold, and 25 parts of alloy. That's fairly pure gold, but of course it's not as pure as the gold in a bar stamped ".999." The closer to the magical "1.000" mark you can come, the better your investment.

Understand, though, that almost no piece of gold today is stamped "1.000." Since no refinery is so exacting that it can eliminate all traces of base metal, gold is almost never designated as being purer than .999, or 999/1,000, gold. For practical purposes, anything stamped ".999" is considered to be pure gold.

Almost no jewelry is that pure, and if you've been familiar with gold up to now chiefly through coins and jewelry, the very term "fineness" may be new to you. A much more common way of designating purity, or quality, of gold is to measure it in terms of karats.

Measuring precious items in karats goes way back to the ancient world, when Arab traders weighed precious stones against *qirats,* or small bean pods, to determine their relative value. As a modern unit of measurement, the karat leaves much to be desired, since it is not terribly exact, and for the close measurements that are needed to distinguish, for example, between .9975 and .999 gold, karats are no good at all. But they do have the weight of tradition behind them and are still widely used today. For that reason, they are important to you as an investor. If you don't understand karats, you will be in the situation of the young man in the Introduction, who purchased a 14-karat ring thinking it was made of pure gold.

Pure, or fine, gold is by definition 24-karat (24-Kt) gold. A karat, simply speaking, is a twenty-fourth part of the whole, and a piece of gold that is twenty-four karats in purity is equivalent to 1.000 fine gold. A karat, then, is a measure not of weight but of fineness. If you want to know how much "pure" gold there is in that white-gold ring you have, look for the karat mark. If it says, "18 Kt," your ring is eighteen parts gold and six parts alloy—or approximately three quarters gold. European jewelers stamp this "750."

Most gold used in jewelry is 18-karat or 14-karat gold. It has to be, because, as I've mentioned, 24-karat (1.000 fine) gold is too soft to be practical for jewelry. You can also find jewelry in 12-karat or even 10-karat purity. You will seldom find a piece of even costume jewelry that is marked less than 10 karat, for the Jewelers Vigilance Committee, which regulates such designations, prohibits jewelers from calling "gold" anything which is less than 10 karats. (That's only 10/24, or 5/12, gold.)

We'll be talking more about karat markings in the chapters on jewelry, later. In this chapter we'll be dealing exclusively with gold of very great fineness—that is, with 24-karat, or nearly 24-karat, gold. This is important to remember, because if you are going to be buying bars or coins or medallions, you need to be sure that your purchase's quality is very high. A 14-karat ring can be very desirable, as long as you know its quality; a 14-karat gold bar is unheard of.

So much for your gold's quality. What about the quantity you are buying?

2. Quantity

Determining a quantity of gold means determining its overall weight —the weight, that is to say, of the gold itself and not of the alloyed object in which the gold is found. That seems like a simple enough matter, but unfortunately for the small investor, goldbugs use a different system of weight measurement than the one we use in everyday life. Our bathroom scales, our postal scales, and our butcher's scales all use the familiar pounds-and-ounces system, which is officially called the *avoirdupois* standard. Precious metals, on the other hand, are measured on the *troy* weight standard.

The basic unit of weight in the troy system is the *troy ounce,* which is about 10 percent heavier than the avoirdupois ounce. Each troy ounce is divided into 20 *pennyweights* (abbreviated dwt), and each pennyweight is further divided into 24 *grains.* A grain is a little less than one fifteenth of a gram, and there are about 454 (to be precise, 453.59) grams in an avoirdupois pound. The accompanying conversion chart should make these terms a little more meaningful to you.

Troy/Avoirdupois Conversion Chart

The following table lists the units of weights and measurements most used in the jewelry trade, together with certain other, related units. Each unit named is followed by its correct abbreviation (in parentheses) and its equivalent in one or more units of the same quantity.

1 carat (c. or ct.) =	0.00705478 oz. av. = 100 points = 0.2 g. = 200 mg. = 3.08647 gr. = 4 pearl grains.
* 1 pennyweight (dwt.) =	0.003428571 lb. av. = 0.0041667 lb. t. = .05 oz. t. = 0.0548571 oz. av. = 24 gr. = 1.55517 g. = 1,555.17 mg.
1 pearl grain =	0.25 ct.
1 kilogram (kg.) =	2.20462 lb. av. = 2.6792285 lb. t. = 32.15076 oz. t. = 35.273957 oz. av. = 643.01 dwt. = 15,432.35639 gr. = 1,000 g.
1 gram (g.) =	0.03527 oz. av. = 0.03215 oz. t. = 0.6430 dwt. = 15.4324 gr. = 0.001 kg. = 5 ct. = 1,000 mg.
1 milligram (mg.) =	0.015432 gr. = 0.001 g. = 0.005 ct.
1 millimeter (mm.) =	0.03937 inch.
1 grain (gr.) =	0.0020833 oz. t. = 0.0022857 oz. av. = 0.041667 dwt. = 0.0648 g. = 0.3240 ct. = 64.798919 mg. (Note: the grain troy equals the grain avoirdupois.)
1 pound troy (lb. t.) =	0.822857 lb. av. = 12 oz. t. = 13.1657 oz. av. = 240 dwt. = 5,760 gr. = 0.3732418 kg. = 373.24177 g. = 1,866.12 cts.
1 ounce troy (oz. t.) =	1.09714 oz. av. = 20 dwt. = 480 gr. = 31.103481 g. = 155.51 ct.
1 pound avoirdupois (lb. av.) =	1.21528 lb. t. = 14.5833 oz. t. = 16 oz. av. = 291.667 dwt. = 7,000 gr. = 0.4535924 kg. = 453.5924 g. = 2267.962 cts.
1 ounce avoirdupois (oz. av.) =	0.9114883 oz. t. = 18.22917 dwt. = 437.5 gr. = 28.3495 g. = 141.75 ct.

* troy weight

How much is a troy ounce of gold? How much gold will you be holding in your hand when you plunk down your $450 or $500 per troy ounce?

Not very much at all. In fact, with gold at $500 an ounce you could easily hold thousands of dollars' worth of the metal in the palm of one hand: at this price, one *avoirdupois* pound would be worth $7,291.65. This, of course, is one of the reasons gold has always been so highly regarded: it is such a dense metal (that is, its weight is so great in relation to its volume) that a little bit goes a long way.

Consider, for example, the most popular gold coin being traded today: the South African Krugerrand. It's a popular way to own gold because it contains exactly one troy ounce of gold, in addition to about a tenth of an ounce of alloy. This coin is only 32.3 millimeters in diameter, or one and a quarter inches. That's about the size of an American half dollar, and at $500 spot gold, it will cost you about $525. That's a great deal of value put into a very tiny package.

You should always know the exact weight of any gold item you purchase, and be able to calculate its value based on the current spot price. That's why we give the conversion tables here. You probably won't need to use them very often, since most reliable dealers list the weights and prices of their gold in both the troy and the metric systems. But it is useful to be able to double-check, to be sure that the price you are paying is exactly the day's going rate and has not been "adjusted" by either an honest error or a fraud. I advise you to carry a calculator and to do your figuring in advance, as soon as you know about how much you will buy.

One further clarification: When you buy and sell gold, the weight that you have to consider is not the weight of the gold object itself, but the weight of the pure gold in that object, or what assayers call its *melt weight:* that's the weight of the pure gold you would get if you melted the object down. There is almost always a difference between overall weight and melt weight. If you are selling a coin that is .900 fine (a standard purity for coins) and the coin weighs exactly one troy ounce, you must not expect to be paid that day's spot price for gold: what you will get in this case is 90 percent of that price, or $450 if gold is at $500 an ounce.

We will talk more about melt values when we consider your options in coins. But let's begin discussing your options by taking first the simplest way to own gold—one in which melt weight is seldom an issue.

OPTION 1: GOLD BULLION

People unfamiliar with the gold market often tend to think of bullion as the exclusive property of millionaires, royalty, oil sheikhs. When they read "bullion," they see piles of shining gold bars stashed in some exotic underground vault and available only to people who pick their teeth with gold toothpicks.

This is an old-fashioned, inaccurate image. "Bullion" is merely a term used to describe any precious metal in bar form, and although in the past most bullion was in the form of very large bars, this is no longer the case. European banks have been selling small units of bullion for decades, and since the 1975 "liberation" of American gold, U.S. banks have too. With so many new, small buyers wanting gold, they have had to make the metal available in units that people can afford. As a result, you now can buy gold bullion in a great range of sizes, going all the way from a 400-ounce London Delivery Bar, which is used in government transactions and futures speculation, down to a one-gram gold "wafer" offered by Crédit Suisse and other banks.

A one-gram wafer of gold, at $500 an ounce, will cost you about seventeen dollars, so that, even when a bank demands that you buy such wafers in lots of ten or more, you can see that it's possible to get into gold buying with quite a small initial investment. In fact, this is one reason that novice goldbugs often prefer to buy bullion. Bullion may sound like Fort Knox, but it's really the least expensive way to own gold.

The reason for this is simple. Bullion is simply a slab of the pure metal, with a minimum of identifying marks. The only writing you will see on a bar or wafer of gold will be the name of the refiner, the weight and fineness numbers, and the certification number of the bar itself. Compare that to the intricate die work that appears on most coins, and you will understand why, compared to coinage, bullion is quite easy to produce. Because of that, you pay a slightly smaller fabrication charge for bullion than you would for a coin, with all its stars, draperies and laurel leaves.

But the relative cheapness of bullion is only one of many reasons that it is attractive to buyers. A second major reason is that, unlike coinage, bullion is nearly pure gold. Its fineness is generally .9995 or slightly less, and virtually all bullion (certainly all bullion you should consider) is at least .995 pure. This makes the calculation of value very simple. In most cases, you don't have to worry about karats and percentages at all. If your bar is one ounce of pure gold, you are paying for no more and no less than that.

In addition, the price of gold bullion is quoted widely throughout the world, so you don't have to worry about a seller quoting you a lower figure than the one you anticipated—it's just too easy for you to check it. Gold bullion is universally recognized, and it is therefore easy to resell. Its liquidity, measured against that of coins, is very high.

Finally, when you buy bullion, you can often avoid paying sales tax on it. Many states do not tax it at all, and even if you live in a state that does, you can easily arrange to take delivery of your purchase in another state and thus avoid the tax. This is perfectly legal, and very commonly done.

Those are the advantages of bullion. Are there any drawbacks?

Well, there is the matter of storage charges and of dealers' commissions. These are the unpleasant facts of buying gold, but since you would have to contend with them in buying any other precious commodity as well, they can hardly be considered unique to bullion. You should expect to pay the bank or broker a commission of a couple of percentage points whenever you buy or sell: don't be surprised if you end up paying 3 or 4 percent. As for storage charges, this brings up the interesting question of whether or not you actually want to hold the gold you buy. Some people like to see and handle their gold, and so they arrange to take delivery, then place the metal in a safe or a safety-deposit box. Safety-deposit boxes, of course, cost money, but if you want to be able physically to handle your investment from time to time, the safety is worth the rental fee. If you prefer to keep it in a home safe, just be sure its loss is insured under your homeowners policy.

Alternatively, you can arrange to have the bank or broker you buy from keep the metal in insured storage for you. You won't get to see it that way, but you will be saved the trouble of arranging storage and insurance yourself. In many cases, moreover, the storage and insurance rates you get from the seller will be slightly lower than those you could get for yourself. Merrill Lynch, which has been selling gold for several years now, even offers its bullion buyers something called a Sharebuilder program, which provides free storage and insurance for a limited period of time.

If you decide to let the bank or broker keep your gold for you, you will receive a *certificate* indicating just what it is you've bought; this certificate will note the refiner's name, the weight and fineness of the bar or wafer and also (this is very important) its unique *number*. Each individual bar and wafer has its own number and corresponding certificate. Having such a certificate is as good as having the gold, since you can "cash it in" at any time either for the gold itself or for its spot-market value in cash. The only real disadvantage of these certificates is that some banks will issue them and store the gold for you only if you buy a certain minimum amount of gold—sometimes as much as ten ounces. If you've only a small amount of money to invest, then, you might have to store it yourself.

If you store it yourself, you will still receive a certificate. If you are not offered one, you should insist on it or look for another dealer. All reliable sellers of gold bullion issue certificates of authenticity. This is proof of their integrity, as well as a guarantee for you.

Assuming you have a fair amount of money to invest, one more thing you will want to consider is the *size* of bullion to buy. The *bar charges* levied on your purchase to cover manufacturing costs will be considerably lower if you purchase a single large bar than if you purchase several smaller ones. Banker Peter Cavelti explains why this is so:

> Generally, it will cost the refiner the same amount of money to manufacture the ten-ounce bar as it costs him to make a one-ounce bar. Consequently, if you purchase ten one-ounce bars, you will pay this charge ten times while if you buy one ten-ounce bar you only pay once.[1]

On the other side of the equation, having a number of smaller units is the more attractive situation if you are investing in gold as an ultimate "crisis hedge." If you want gold as a liquid currency in the case of a national or international collapse, the ten 1-ounce bars make more sense. Having the one 10-ounce bar would put you in the unenviable position of the man with the million-dollar check: it's not much good to him unless somebody can give him change. Small bars would also be better in a barter situation.

How much gold you buy, therefore, and in what form you buy it, are largely a matter of your own financial tastes and political expectations. This is even more blatantly the case with the next option.

OPTION 2: COINS AND MEDALLIONS

Many people, considering bullion an unimaginative (if sound) way of owning gold, prefer to put their money into gold coins or medallions. Many gold coins, of course, are items of very great beauty, and this beauty accounts for their popularity among many new entrants into the gold market.

[1] See Cavelti, *How to Invest in Gold*, p. 71.

But beauty must be paid for, and when you buy gold coins, you will be paying a higher fee for them per ounce than you would if you bought an equivalent amount of straight bullion. The difference between the melt value of a coin (the value of the pure gold in it) and the price you pay for the coin is known among collectors as the *premium*. If you invest in gold coins, you will pay this premium for the added attractions they offer.

The premium can vary considerably, not only from dealer to dealer but also from coin to coin. It is always highest, however, on those coins which have, in addition to their gold bullion value, some artistic or historical feature that makes them of interest to collectors. These coins, which are the most highly prized (and highly priced), are known as *numismatic* coins. They are the top of the line in coin collecting.

1. Numismatic Coins

The history of coin collecting is nearly as old as coinage itself. The Roman historian Pliny, writing in the first century A.D., mentioned not only several famous collections, but also the prevalence of forgeries—so it is evident that the attraction and the hazards of numismatics have been known for some time. In recent years, coin collecting has grown considerably in popularity, and this has had the effect of making coins that were already valuable even more highly prized. More people are demanding old coins, but there is a limited supply, so the prices keep going up. Since this trend is likely to continue, you would be well advised (assuming you are attracted to coins in the first place) to think about buying gold in this way.

The world of modern numismatics is a complicated and often hazardous one, and I would not presume to advise you here on making specific purchases. If you are anxious to trade in numismatics, the first thing you should do is to get a reliable guide (such as the 1982 *Investors Guide: Gold Bullion and Coins,* published by Dell Books) and also check out recent issues of the trade publications *Numismatic News* and *Coin World.* Only by familiarizing yourself with current prices and offers can you be assured of avoiding trouble.

In addition, you should recognize a few basic guidelines that the big-time coin collectors follow. Investing in numismatic gold is something like investing in art or antiques. What the professional looks for, basically, are *age, rarity* and *condition*.

Age and rarity often, but not always, go together. Generally speaking, the earlier a coin was minted, the fewer examples will be around today. This is because the striking methods were more primitive years ago, and the dies used to strike the coins were more fragile than our own. So if you find a gold coin that is a couple of hundred years old, it is probably going to be worth more than one minted sixty years ago. Coins from the ancient world, for this reason, are the most valuable of all.

But this general rule is subject to modifications. The production of coins, like the production of any commodity, fluctuates in response to various economic factors, and for that reason the connection between age and rarity is far from exact. What a collector wants to know is the precise year and place in which the coin was minted. Collectors favor coins of low mintages, and grade the desirability of their coins in terms of specific dates. Years in which mint numbers were especially low are called key dates, years in which they were moderately low are called semikey dates and years in which they were normal or high are called common dates. A common date for a particular coin may be more recent than a key date, but it may also be a great deal older.

In addition, coins produced in smaller mintages often command a better price than those produced in larger numbers—again, because of their relative rarity. In 1982, for example, a $2.50 gold piece minted in Denver in 1840 was selling for $2,000. One produced fourteen years *later* in San Francisco was selling for $52,500, simply because the Denver mintage was 3,500 and the San Francisco one only 256.

But age and rarity are only the beginning. No matter how old or how rare a coin is, it will be of almost no interest to a collector unless it is also in very good condition. Even a key-date coin will be deflated in value if it is nicked, worn, or in some other way defaced. The most discriminating collectors will not even look at coins that are not in mint condition, and even the smaller collectors insist on the next-highest grades. The following chart will indicate how picky collectors can be about the grading of their coins. Condition is of such importance in this field that coin dealers, when they advertise their stock, always list grades as well as dates. (Of course, one dealer's VF may be another one's F, so it is important to be able to *see* any coins in which you're interested before you agree to buy.)

Numismatic Coin Grades

Essential elements of the American Numismatic Association (ANA) grading system:

PROOF – A specially made coin distinguished by sharpness of detail and usually with a brilliant, mirrorlike surface. Proof refers to the method of manufacture and is not a condition, but normally the term implies perfect mint state unless otherwise noted and graded as below.

MINT STATE – The terms mint state (MS) and uncirculated (unc.) are interchangeably used to describe coins showing no trace of wear. Such coins may vary to some degree because of blemishes, toning or slight imperfections as described in the following subdivisions.

PERFECT UNCIRCULATED (MS-70) – Perfect new condition, showing no trace of wear. The finest quality possible, with no evidence of scratches, handling or contact with other coins. Very few regular-issue coins are ever found in this condition.

CHOICE UNCIRCULATED (MS-65) – An above-average uncirculated coin which may be brilliant or lightly toned and has very few contact marks on the surface or rim. MS-67 or MS-63 indicates a slightly higher or lower grade of preservation.

UNCIRCULATED (MS-60) – Has no trace of wear but may show a number of contact marks, and the surface may be spotted or lack some luster.

CHOICE ABOUT UNCIRCULATED (AU-55) – Barest evidence of light wear on only the highest points of the design. Most of the mint luster remains.

ABOUT UNCIRCULATED (AU-50) – Has traces of light wear on many of the high points. At least half of the mint luster is still present.

CHOICE EXTREMELY FINE (EF-45) – Light overall wear shows on highest points. All design details are very sharp. Some of the mint luster is evident.

EXTREMELY FINE (EF-40) – Design is lightly worn throughout, but all features are sharp and well defined. Traces of luster may show.

CHOICE VERY FINE (VF-30) – Light, even wear on the surface and highest parts of the design. All lettering and major features are sharp.

VERY FINE (VF-20) – Shows moderate wear on high points of design. All major details are clear.

FINE (F-12) – Moderate to considerable even wear. Entire design is bold, with overall pleasing appearance.

VERY GOOD (VG-8) – Well worn, with main features clear and bold although rather flat.

GOOD (G-4) – Heavily worn, with design visible but faint in areas. Many details are flat.

ABOUT GOOD (AG-3) – Very heavily worn, with portions of lettering, date and legends worn smooth. The date may be barely readable.

Note: Damaged coins, such as those which are bent, corroded, scratched, holed, nicked, stained or mutilated, are worth less than those without defects. Slightly worn coins ("sliders") that have been cleaned and conditioned ("whizzed") to simulate uncirculated luster are worth considerably less than perfect pieces. Unlike damage inflicted after striking, manufacturing defects do not always lessen values.

The premium you pay for a coin will be in direct proportion to its rarity and its condition. In the case of numismatic gold coins, that premium can be extraordinarily high—so high that the selling price of the coin will have little to do with the value of its bullion content. The collectors, remember, are paying for history and beauty. The premium paid for these features may cause a small gold coin to sell for tens or even hundreds of times the value of the bullion of which it's made. That San Francisco gold piece, for example—the one that sold for $52,500— probably had a melt value of about $62.50.

It should be clear by now that, when you buy numismatic gold, you are not really investing in gold per se—not in the same, direct way you would be if you purchased wafers or bars. The melt value of a numismatic coin is merely its *minimum* value—the value you would get for it if you were foolish enough to melt it down. This is an important fact, because the value you realize from numismatics is only marginally connected with the fluctuating world price of gold. What you are paying for here is the premium. This becomes more obvious as the value of your purchase rises: the more expensive the coin, the less its value is dependent on the spot price of the metal.

Take a hypothetical one-ounce gold coin of which 90 percent by weight is pure gold. (This is a common percentage in coins—so much so that .900 fine gold is commonly referred to as "coin gold.") That means that the intrinsic, or melt, value of the coin, assuming gold is at $500, is 90 percent of that figure, or $450.

Say the coin is a common-date, VF specimen that sells for $600. The premium, then, would be $150, or the difference between the melt value and the selling price. If the price of gold suddenly dropped to $200, what would happen to the value of the coin? The intrinsic value would drop to $180, the premium would remain at about $150, and the new value of the coin would be $330.

But now say that the coin is a key-date, uncirculated specimen that sells for $5,000. The intrinsic value of the coin would, again, be $450, but the premium would be the difference between that and $5,000, or

$4,550. With a coin of this high a premium, even if the gold price dropped to $200 (the intrinsic value to $180), you would still be able to sell the coin for $4,730. You would have lost $270 on the spot-price drop but retained the bulk of the coin's value. The percentage of loss, in other words, gets less as the numismatic premium goes up. That's why the big-time collectors are not exceptionally worried about the day-to-day prices of gold: their investment is not tied to melt value. In fact, it is even possible for the value of a key-date coin to *advance* when the price of bullion is declining.

But this observation is true only for coins of a certain quality. As I've mentioned, many collectors will not touch coins that have circulated widely; the greater the wear on a coin, the more drastically the premium drops. If a coin is severely worn, it may have no numismatic value at all and may thus bring a market price at or near the melt value. In such a case, the coin will have ceased to be a numismatic investment and become what is termed a purely "bullion" one.

Coins without numismatic value are not of much interest to collectors, but that definitely does not mean they are worthless. On the contrary, buying and selling coins for their melt value alone can be a rewarding and lucrative business.

2. Bullion Coins

As you will have surmised from the previous section, investing in numismatic coins can be a very expensive "hobby." Because of the enormous premiums charged for unworn and rare coins, the novice investor might have a hard time getting started in this area. In addition, unless you are willing to do fairly intensive research into numismatics, you are in danger of losing out to those with more experience and knowledge. For these reasons, investing in numismatic coins is still pretty much a specialist's endeavor.

Not so with bullion coins. The two chief advantages of investing in bullion coins are that a) they are nearly as cheap to own as plain bar bullion and b) you do not have to be a coin expert to invest profitably in them. For the novice investor with little risk capital, these coins are tailor-made. You do have to pay a premium on them, but it is nominal compared to that on numismatics, and assuming that you keep your bullion coins in good condition, you will probably be able to recoup the premium when you resell (ask your dealer about this before you buy).

Bullion coins, by definition, are coins whose value is the same, or very nearly the same, as the intrinsic value of their metal. They are coins, in other words, that you buy for the simple reason that they are made of gold.

I mentioned that an old numismatic, if it is badly worn, can "become" a bullion coin by losing its extrinsic value to collectors. Most bullion coins are not made in this way, however; they are born as bullion coins. They are mint-fresh new coins manufactured specifically for investors. Unlike the numismatics, they were never intended to serve as negotiable currency, and even though some of them are stamped with currency values, these are largely symbolic: a Canadian Maple Leaf stamped "$50" for example, is worth much more than that. The intended use of these coins is as investment vehicles.

Because this is so, most of the current bullion coins are extremely pure in quality and of weights that make it easy to determine quickly how much each is worth. The very popular South African Krugerrand, for example, contains exactly one troy ounce of gold—as does the Canadian Maple Leaf. Both of these coins are thus readily negotiable, since, being struck by contemporary governments, their weight, fineness and gold content are all very closely regulated. Owning a Maple Leaf or a Krugerrand, then, is as good as owning straight bullion.

These two coins, moreover, are only the top of the line. The Krugerrand is especially popular, with over 20 million having been sold since it was first minted, in 1967. But any currency or coin dealer will be able to give you a selection of bullion coins that includes not only these front runners, but also such other reliable issues as the Mexican 50-peso piece and the Austrian and Hungarian 100 coronas. See the chart below for my selection of your best buys in bullion coins.

Best Coin Buys

United States—Original Issues
  $20 "DOUBLE EAGLE" St. Gaudens type, 1907–33
  Fine gold content: .9675 oz.
  $20 "DOUBLE EAGLE" Liberty type, 1850–1907
  Fine gold content: .9675 oz.
  $10 "EAGLE" Indian Head type, 1907–33
  Fine gold content: .4838 oz.
  $10 "EAGLE" Liberty type, 1839–1907
  Fine gold content: .4838 oz.
  $5 "HALF EAGLE" Indian Head type, 1908–29
  Fine gold content: .2419 oz.
  $5 "HALF EAGLE" Liberty type, 1840–1908
  Fine gold content: .2419 oz.
  $3 LIBERTY HEAD, 1854–89
  Fine gold content: .1449 oz.

$2.50 "QUARTER EAGLE" Indian Head type, 1908–29
Fine gold content: .1209 oz.
$2.50 "QUARTER EAGLE" Liberty type, 1840–1907
Fine gold content: .1209 oz.
$1 LIBERTY HEAD (large), 1856–89
Fine gold content: .0483 oz.
$1 LIBERTY HEAD (small), 1849–54
Fine gold content: .0483 oz.

England—Original Issues
ONE-POUND PIECES (also known as sovereigns)
Fine gold content: .2354 oz.
VICTORIA—Young Head, 1871–85
VICTORIA—Jubilee Head, 1877–92
VICTORIA—Old Head, 1893–1901
EDWARD VII, 1902–10
GEORGE V, 1911–25
ELIZABETH II, 1957–74

France—Original Issues
20-FRANC PIECES (also called Napoleons)
Fine gold content: .1867 oz.
NAPOLEON III, 1853–70
ANGEL WRITING, 1871–98
REPUBLIC HEAD, 1899–1915

Switzerland—Original Issue
20 FRANCS "Vreneli," 1897–1933
Fine gold content: .1867 oz.

Belgium—Original Issue
20 FRANCS LEOPOLD II, 1866–82
Fine gold content: .1867 oz.

Austria—Official Government Restrikes
100 CORONAS, 1915
Fine gold content: .9802 oz.
20 CORONAS, 1915
Fine gold content: .1960 oz.
10 CORONAS, 1912
Fine gold content: .0980 oz.
8 FLORINS, 1892
Fine gold content: .1864 oz.
4 DUCATS, 1915

Fine gold content: .4429 oz.
1 DUCAT, 1915
Fine gold content: .1107 oz.

Netherlands—Original Issue
10 GUILDERS, various dates
Fine gold content: .1946 oz.

Canada—Original Issue
$50 "MAPLE LEAF," 1979
Fine gold content: 1 oz.

Turkey—Original Issue
100 PIASTRES, various dates
Fine gold content: .2127 oz.

Colombia—Original Issue
5 PESOS
STONE CUTTER; SMALL, LARGE HEAD, 1903–30
Fine gold content: .2354 oz.

South Africa—Original Issue
KRUGERRAND, 1967 to date
Fine gold content: 1 oz.

Mexico—Official Government Restrikes
50 PESOS, 1947
Fine gold content: 1.2057 oz.
20 PESOS, 1959
Fine gold content: .4823 oz.
10 PESOS, 1959
Fine gold content: .2412 oz.

You should shop around from dealer to dealer when buying and selling bullion coins, since dealers' premiums vary slightly. And you should compare coin values, to be sure you are getting the most gold you can buy for your money. The principal thing to determine here is that the price you pay per ounce is as close as possible to the current spot price of gold. Since there is no numismatic value to a bullion coin, you should not readily pay more than 4 or 5 percent over the melt value as a premium.

In order to determine how much you are paying per ounce, you first need to know how much gold is in a given coin. Any good dealer will have this information available, and I have included the gold content information for my best buys in the chart. You will note there that the Krugerrand, although it is slightly heavier than the Maple Leaf, contains precisely the same amount of gold: one troy ounce. Thus it should retail for about the same price. It is the weight of the gold alone that is important, not the total weight or the supposed "artistic" value of the coin. Krugerrands and their kin are simply too widespread today to have any such extrinsic value to a collector. That is why their premiums are so low. When Krugerrands were first placed on the market, the premium was 20 percent. This is now 3 percent, according to Alan Posnick, of Manfra Tordella & Brookes Inc., 59 West 49th Street, New York City. He finds that the Maple Leaf and the Krugerrand are the most popular. However, he points out the Austrian 100-corona is sold closest to spot, with a premium of close to 1 percent.

3. Restrikes

A *restrike* is a reminting of an old coin, struck with the original die or one identical to it—a copy, in other words, of an old coin. An *offstrike* takes this copying one step further: it's a restrike done in a metal other than the one originally used—such as a modern gold copy of a silver original.

Restrikes are issued for several reasons. One is to take advantage of the popularity of rare numismatics: restriking one of these rarities can make it available to many more people, and even though that reduces the value of the original, it's good economics for the minting government. Second, restrikes satisfy, at a reasonable cost, the increasing demand for bullion coins. And third, they flatter the national pride of the minter: many restrikes are reissues of famous old patriotic coins.[2]

There is nothing really wrong with restriking, as long as it's done aboveboard. There are many handsome restrikes available today, and as you will note from the Best Coin Buys chart, some of them are exceptional bargains in terms of their bullion value. The Hungarian Government does a great many restrikes, and its current reissue of the 100-corona gold piece is an example of bullion minting at its best.

The problems with buying restrikes is that, in some cases, a government will conceal the fact that the coin is a restrike, rather than an original. Few restrikes have marks distinguishing them as such. Since the amount of pure gold in a restrike is identical to that in the original, this makes no difference in terms of bullion value. But it can make an appreciable difference indeed in terms of real or supposed numismatic value.

[2] See Donald Hoppe, *How to Invest in Gold Coins.*

A restrike, strictly speaking, has no numismatic value. But what is to prevent an unscrupulous dealer from passing off one of these copies as an original, and charging a huge numismatic premium for it? Not very much, I'm afraid—and this is the inherent danger in purchasing coins of high numismatic value. A restrike is a kind of *tertium quid* between true numismatics and bullion coins. It looks and feels like an antique, but its value is only that of a copy. That's where the trouble arises.

When you are buying coins, therefore, you are like the furniture buyer who takes the copy of the Louis XV chair convinced that it's an original. Anyone trying to sell you a copy of an antique as an original will, of course, give you plenty of assurances—but how can you be sure they are genuine? Since it is next to impossible to distinguish between most restrikes and their originals, you are always on tricky ground here. Therefore, whenever you are offered a supposed original of a coin that you suspect may be a restrike (see the list of common restrikes on this page), I'd advise you to pass it up unless you are absolutely certain of your seller. Pay the bullion value, plus a small commission, but do not lay down a numismatic premium for something that could easily turn out to be a copy. That way, if it does turn out to be a copy, you have still paid a fair price for it. If it turns out to be an original, you are that much ahead.

Common Restrikes

Mexico

50 pesos	1947
20 pesos	1959
10 pesos	1959

Austria

100 coronas	1915
20 coronas	1915
10 coronas	1912
4 ducats	1915
1 ducat	1915
8 florins	1892

4. Medallions

You should exercise similar caution when you are shopping for medals or medallions. A medal is a metal memento of a person or an event; a medallion is a large-size medal. There are some fine examples of these commemorative pieces being produced today, both by governments and by such private concerns as the Franklin Mint, but you should keep in mind, if you are interested in them as investments, that the metal you get for your money is very much less than you would get from a bullion coin of the same size. Always check the gold content before buying, and you will usually find that the premium above melt value is quite high.

That doesn't mean you should forget about them entirely. If a given medal interests you—if it has the same kind of artistic merit or historical value you would look for in a numismatic—then by all means investigate it. But look at it in the same way that you would look at a numismatic coin: expect to pay a hefty premium, and do not fool yourself into thinking that you are investing in fine gold.

Medals, like numismatics, are of interest primarily to collectors. That is why so many of them are issued in sets and limited editions. You should remember that the larger an edition, the less exclusive it will be and therefore the less valuable. Keep in mind as well that no serious collector will be interested in a set that is missing one or more pieces. If you intend to buy the Franklin Mint's latest series of medallions, plan to buy the entire series.

A last word on buying coins and medallions. Remember that, like bullion bars and wafers, coins and medallions involve certain inevitable extra charges, possible inconveniences, and risks, and you should be alert to them if you are to trade wisely in this area. What I have already said about taking good physical care of your bullion, and of keeping it in an insured storage space, goes for medals and coins as well. A principal asset of these items is their beauty, and the only ones that you can expect to resell without question are those which have never been removed from their sealed protective cases. As with bullion, you will have to pay sales taxes, and as with bullion, you can arrange to have the seller keep the physical coins and just issue you a certificate. Be sure you get a certificate, too, even if you accept delivery.

To be realistic, do not count on receiving more than 90 percent of the melt value of a medal or medallion on the day you decide to sell. This 10 percent difference is the cost of refining into fine gold plus the profit of the dealer.

OPTION 3: GOLD FUTURES

The question of whether or not to accept delivery of the actual gold is an open one in bullion and coins. In gold futures trading, that question is virtually closed, because in this curious gold market, practically no buyer ever receives his or her gold. The whole point of futures in gold, in fact, is to terminate your agreement to buy before you are required to pay.

I know that may sound odd, and the gold futures market is indeed an odd market. Here's how it works.

Gold futures trading is done in the commodity markets, just like trading in soybean or sowbelly futures. In North America, the major three commodity markets are the International Monetary Market, in Chicago; the Commodity Exchange, in New York; and the Winnepeg Commodity Exchange, in Manitoba. When you are dealing in gold futures, you make a contract through a commodities broker at one of these exchanges. In the contract, you agree to buy, at a designated future date, a stipulated amount of gold at a stipulated price. At the time you do so, you are required to put down a certain percentage, or *margin* (usually 10 percent), to ensure the sale. You don't have to pay the remainder until the due date of the contract.

The attraction of a futures contract is that it effectively freezes the price of a fluctuating commodity and thus enables you to plan ahead without worrying about future rises or falls. This is particularly useful to people in industry—jewelers, for example—who want to take delivery of gold at some point in the future but want to lock in a price for it now.

Let's look at an example. Say you are a jewelry manufacturer. It is now January and you know from your advance orders that by April you will need a hundred ounces of gold. The gold price has been on the rise, however, and you don't want to take the chance that by April it will be too high for you to afford. To protect yourself from this contingency of rising prices, you purchase an April futures contract for your one hundred ounces of gold, at a price that is above the current spot price, but below the price you anticipate it will go to in April.

Say the current spot price is $450 and you fear that, by April, when you need the gold, it will go to $550. You might ask your broker to sell you a futures contract at $459, for delivery in April. You put down a 10 percent margin (in this case, $4,590) plus a commission (about 1% or less), and make your budget plans accordingly. You know that, no matter how high gold goes, you have a guaranteed shipment for your needs at a price that you can live with.

Between now and April, the price could either rise or fall. If it goes to $550 or $560, you can congratulate yourself: you will have *hedged* successfully and saved the difference per ounce between the $459 you agreed upon and the higher, April price. If by April gold goes to $560, for example, you will have saved $101 an ounce, or $10,100. If the price goes down, you will be confronted by the unpleasant realization that you have lost out on a windfall profit—but that will be a small consideration compared to knowing that your resource needs are met and that you have budgeted wisely based on that livable $459-per-ounce price.

Such a consideration is not small, however, to most of the players in the futures game. Most of the players are not small manufacturers, but speculators who see in the fluctuating price of gold an opportunity for quick killings. To a speculator, the usual kind of transaction is not a hedge, but an *offset* transaction. Here's how it works.

Say you as a speculator feel that the price of gold in April will be significantly higher than it is today. To make a profit in futures on that rise, you tell your broker to "go long" on one hundred ounces of the metal: that is, to buy one hundred ounces for you for April delivery, say at that same $459 price. You pay the $4,590 margin, plus commission, and, just like the hedger, watch what happens to the price. If it goes above $459 at any time before the delivery date, you can sell your April contract at the going rate: if the April price rises to $500, you will have made a $4,100 profit, and the buyer will have assumed the April promise—speculating on the hope that, before April, the price will rise even further. In this kind of transaction, in which you liquidate the original contract, a speculator who never sees any physical gold can make a very tidy profit, or take a big loss if he has guessed wrong.

You can even profit in the futures market when the gold price is falling. In this kind of situation, you tell your broker to "go short," that is, to sell a futures contract, again for delivery in April. You do this when you feel the price will be significantly lower in April than it is now; you are betting on the possibility that, before April, the price will go so low that you will be able to buy the gold you have promised to deliver and simultaneously liquidate your futures contract by selling it at a profit to another speculator. You are hoping, for example, that gold will drop to $420 in March: then you can offset your promised sale by the purchase of an equal amount of gold, but at a lower price. In this situation, in the wry words of Peter Cavelti, "You don't actually have to deliver the gold. Yours has been purely a paper transaction. But the profits you have made, the difference between the price you sold gold at and the price you paid to repurchase it, are real."[3]

The vast majority of gold futures contracts are settled in this manner. Over 95 percent of them are offset, rather than being carried through to delivery. This is true largely because many futures participants are not hedgers, but speculators, whose interest in gold has nothing at all to do

[3] Cavelti, op. cit., p. 97.

with the element's usefulness. The speculators in the futures market are concerned only with gold's price, and it is because of their involvement that that price fluctuates so dramatically. It is because of their involvement that great fortunes are made (and lost) there.

Both speculators and hedgers are necessary for the proper functioning of the market. In the words of the International Monetary Market:

> If the futures market provided no economic function for the hedger, there would be less need for it to exist; and without the speculator to assume the hedger's risk, there would be no market. Together they provide the needed liquidity to facilitate entry into and egress from the market.[4]

Note the words "risk" and "liquidity." Futures trading is definitely not a surefire way to make money. Because of the volatility of the gold price, the extreme activity of trading, and the uncertainty about finding a buyer or seller at the moment you need one at the price you desire, gold futures trading is anything but a sure road to riches. Futures trading can be an exciting and lucrative way of owning gold, but I do not advise it for the fainthearted or for anyone with limited risk capital. Indeed, unless you have a fair amount of assets to begin with, it is unlikely you will even be able to get into futures trading: The minimum futures contract in gold is for 100 troy ounces, which at a spot price of $450 would cost you $45,000. The margin on that would be $4,500— just for getting your foot in the door. Depending on the fluctuating price, moreover, that margin can be raised before the due date, at your broker's discretion.

Anyone seriously contemplating gold futures trading today should contact a reliable commodities broker first and also do some background reading. Peter Cavelti's book *How to Invest in Gold* gives a good survey of the dangers involved in this field, and you can also write to the various commodities exchanges for their free information. The International Monetary Market's brochure mentioned in footnote 4, for example, is available from the IMM at 444 West Jackson Boulevard, Chicago, Illinois 60606.

Futures trading is a much less direct method of "owning" gold than either bullion or coins. For those of you who don't mind dealing in gold merely on paper, it can be a good option—provided you have the entry money and do not overextend yourself. The same thing can be said for various other indirect methods of owning gold. If you simply want gold on paper, you might want to investigate these other options. The princi-

---

[4] See the IMM brochure "Understanding Trading in Gold Futures," Chicago Mercantile Exchange, 1978.

pal "paper gold" options, in addition to futures trading, would be to invest in a gold bullion *fund* or to buy *stocks* in a gold-mining firm.

I won't discuss these options at length, because they are in a sense tangential to the buying and selling of the metal itself. A gold bullion fund, like any investment fund, is managed by professionals, not by you, and that means that, if you invest in such a fund, you are investing not so much in gold as in the managers' expertise. The same thing goes for mining stocks: when you purchase stocks in a gold mine, you are investing not only in gold, but in the business acumen of the owners and managers of the mine. No matter how much gold rises in price, you cannot make a profit on it unless the company is well run.

If you prefer to have your investments managed for you, these indirect methods may be suitable. If you prefer to deal in the metal itself (or certificates for the metal), investing in bullion or coins is probably your best bet.

Whichever option you choose, however, you will need to proceed with care. Whether you have $500 or $50,000 to invest, you need to approach your options like a smart, budget-wise shopper.

CHAPTER 3
THE SMART GOLD SHOPPER

Now that you know the gold investment opportunities available to you, you need to know what to look for and what to look *out* for when you are actually ready to make a deal. If you're going to invest in the Cadillac of metals, you need to do so in a deliberate and cautious manner. You can't rely on the erroneous assumption that as long as it's gold, it's all right. You have to approach every sale carefully, lest you end up paying a fancy price for a lemon.

There are plenty of lemons in the gold investment field, and this chapter is designed to guide you safely past them, so that when you pocket the keys to your safety-deposit box, you know exactly what you've locked inside.

The first thing you need to know is where to shop for your gold. Just as not all Cadillac dealers are alike, so too not all gold dealers are alike. A great many of those who sell gold are steady, reliable business people, but because a certain percentage are not, you have to be on your guard. To spot the cheats before they spot you, you should do some comparison shopping.

SHOPPING AROUND

Before gold was "deregulated" by the federal government in 1975, there were only a few places where the average citizen could buy gold—and the choices were jewelry and numismatic coins. Pawnshops would sell you a ring with eight dollars' worth of gold in it for the "bargain" rate of twenty-five dollars. Coin shops would sell you pre-1933 coins. And you could pick up some items at auctions. But that was about the limit. Since private citizens were not permitted to own gold, the only alternative to the hockshops and the auction circuit for the hungry gold investor was the black-market sources which flourish in any economy where purchasing power is restricted.

In 1975 that all changed. Since then, U.S. citizens have been permitted to own gold, and this has created a huge new network of gold dealers. The pawnshops and auctioneers are still in business, but they now have to compete with more "respectable" outlets such as banks, brokerage houses and the federal government itself. For the person wanting to own gold, there has never been a more "open" time. With a few hundred dollars to spend, you now have access not only to the traditional coin and jewelry outlets, but to a host of infant concerns that will sell you bullion as well.

What are the major outlets for gold trading? We've already mentioned that, for trading in gold futures, you need to contact a commodities broker who is registered with one of the big exchanges. That's the only way you can trade in futures. If you're interested in the less glamorous (and less risky) options of bullion and coin investment, your outlets are considerably more varied. These are the major ones:

1. Banks
Since 1975, many of the country's major banks have been selling both bullion bars and coins such as the Krugerrand and the Maple Leaf. Among the more well-known banks that offer this service at many of their national branches are Citibank, First National Bank of Chicago, Republic National Bank of New York and Swiss Bank Corporation (also of New York). This is only a partial listing; you should check with your own bank to see which banks in your area deal in bullion and coins.

2. Brokerage Houses
One of the more interesting areas of diversification that has hit the brokerage business since 1975 is trading in precious metals. We have already noted that Merrill Lynch will not only sell you bullion (coins and bars) at a modest premium, but that they will store it for you temporarily, cost free. Other brokerage houses may offer similar services; most of the big ones sell gold.

3. Dealers
Banks and brokerage houses deal only in bullion and bullion certificates. Gold dealers, on the other hand, carry a full range of gold items, from bars and wafers to newly minted bullion coins to ancient and rare numismatics. The New York firm of Manfra Tordella & Brookes, Inc., for example, offers its customers not only a wide variety of bars but also a full range of U.S. gold coins, foreign coins, restrikes and medallions. The advantage of using a dealer, rather than a bank or a broker, is that his or her inventory is likely to be larger—and your options will therefore be wider.

But there are dangers in buying from dealers that do not usually arise when you buy from brokers or banks. Not all gold dealers have the experience and reputation of Manfra Tordella & Brookes, and some of them are little more than clip joints set up overnight to take advantage of the public's interest in gold. That is why, when you buy gold of any kind from a dealer, it is worth your while to do some checking beforehand.

Don't be afraid to ask the Better Business Bureau in your area to confirm the reputation of your prospective seller, and don't be so quick to make a deal that you buy from the first dealer you meet. Dealers' premiums and other charges can vary quite a lot (especially on numismatics), so it is to your benefit to compare a number of dealers before you make your purchase. That way, you will avoid paying $500 for an item that you discover the next day is selling for $455 a block away.

Comparison shopping for a reputable dealer can be a tricky and exasperating business, since so many fly-by-night operators have gotten into gold since 1975. To help you in your selection, I have listed a number of good dealers below. None of these will nickel-and-dime you to death with charges or lie about what they are selling. Consult this list before you buy. Obviously it doesn't list every reliable dealer in the country, but it is a reasonable selection of those with the most readily verifiable reputations.

One special firm deserves mention. Johnson Mathey & Wallace Inc., One World Trade Center, New York, N.Y. 10048, is a subsidiary of a 160-year-old company. They are the only large refiners who offer a definite buy-back guarantee. Their charges over spot range from 2 percent for a $5,000 purchase to 1½ percent for amounts over $50,000. Their selling commissions are at the same rates. This means that if you buy $5,000 in gold, you will pay $100 over spot. When you decide to sell, they will pay you spot less 2 percent. You may hold the metal yourself, or they will store your gold fully insured for ½ of 1 percent of the dollar value per annum. They have a complete managed-account commodity program. You can write them for details.

Coin Dealers

Bowers & Merena Inc.
Box 1224
Wolfeboro, N.H. 03894

Brigandi Coin Co.
60 West 44th Street
New York, N.Y. 10036

Joel D. Coen Inc.
39 West 55th Street
New York, N.Y. 10019

Deak-Perera
630 5th Avenue
New York, N.Y. 10020

Galerie des Monnaies of Geneva Ltd.
347 Madison Avenue
New York, N.Y. 10017
(branches in Geneva, Düsseldorf and Paris)

Harmer Rooke
3 East 57th Street
New York, N.Y. 10022

Kagins Numismatic Auctions
1000 Insurance Exchange Bldg.
Des Moines, Ia. 50309

Jules J. Karp Inc.
372 7th Avenue
New York, N.Y. 10001

Manfra Tordella & Brookes Inc.
59 West 49th Street
New York, N.Y. 10020

Republic National Bank of New York
452 5th Avenue
New York, N.Y. 10018

Benjamin Stack
123 West 57th Street
New York, N.Y. 10019

4. Mail-Order Houses

Caution in selecting a dealer goes double when you buy by mail. Mail-order houses have been multiplying like amoebae in recent years, and like amoebae, they ingest "food" (in their case, your money) at an alarmingly rapid rate. Be very careful of any dealer who sells gold exclusively through the mail. Not all of them are dishonest (Manfra Tordella & Brookes, in fact, has a large mail-order operation), but when you buy by mail you're taking chances, because you don't get a chance to inspect your purchases ahead of time. You wouldn't buy a car this way, and unless the firm is well established and offers a money-back guarantee if you are not satisfied, you should also be wary of buying gold this way.

We've all seen the newspaper ads that promise you a "stunning" gold pendant or medallion for a mere $19.95. Putting down that much money for a piece of "real" or "solid" gold may seem like an attractive proposition, but what the ads don't tell you is that the amount of gold in the piece is worth about two dollars in melt value. You are paying for the privilege of owning gold, not for the metal itself. I'll talk more about this in the chapter on the cost of workmanship. For now, just keep in mind that buying gold through newspaper or magazine ads is almost always a risky venture.

5. Jewelers, Pawnshops and Auctions

What about the old standbys: jewelers, pawnbrokers and auctioneers? It's hard to make a blanket statement about these smaller suppliers, but in general it's fair to say that, however fair their sales policies may be, the smaller firms are less likely to give you a competitive price for your purchases than those who can trade in greater bulk: that's a result of the economies of scale. In addition, there are specific drawbacks to dealing with any of these traditional sources. Jewelers take a heavy markup on their gold in order to stay in business, and that markup is passed on to you. Pawnbrokers make their living by buying low and selling high, and there is no way small gold traders can come out ahead in that game. As for auctions, assuming that they have been well advertised beforehand, it isn't terribly likely that they will be a source of real bargains. Auctioned bullion would simply command the day's spot price, while numismatics or jewelry finds would go to the high-rolling bidders—those with the infinitely stretchable pockets of collectors. (In addition, most auction houses set a reserve price on each item. Unless the bids exceed this reserve, the item goes back to the owner. This effectively prevents you from getting a "steal.")

The same principle would of course apply to other outlets for "collectible" gold, such as coin collectors' conventions and ads in the coin magazines. The sad fact about jewelry and numismatic gold is that there are few true bargains to be had. If you are offered a rare old coin at what appears to be a rock-bottom price, the chances are very good that it is either a restrike or a forgery. The values of the choicest old coins are too well known to make the lucky buy more than a rare occurrence.

Of course this is also true of nonnumismatic gold. Wherever you shop, don't expect to make an overnight killing on the spot price. Compare various dealers and other sources, and pick the one that offers you both a premium scale you can live with and a reputation for fair dealing.

How can you spot such a reputation? Or, putting the question in reverse, how do you know when you are not being dealt with fairly?

Obviously there's no surefire way to tell this; if there were, no one would ever get cheated. But there are a few common danger areas to watch out for, a few gold dealers' "tricks" that are used again and again. Knowing what these are may help to make you a more cautious shopper.

TRICKS OF THE TRADE

Since 1975, as I've mentioned, the number of people buying and selling gold has multiplied enormously. There is now an "authorized" gold dealer in almost every shopping center in the country, and more going into and out of business every day. Many of these new operations are honest enough (if somewhat inexperienced), but a fair proportion of them are not. What if you run across one of the latter? What if you decide, for convenience or other reasons, to ignore the bank or brokerage house and go to a small retail shop? What can you expect to find?

My basic advice is to stay away from these "bucket shops" altogether. But I know from experience that some of you will ignore that precept. You will be steered to Friendly Fred's by an obliging relative, the proximity of his shop, or an attractive newspaper ad. Once under his roof, you will be impressed by the opportunities he offers, and quickly be ready to hock your house and your car if only he will give you a shot at that "once in a lifetime" deal.

For those of you in that situation, the following discussion should be helpful. It's a discussion of the most common abuses you may discover (or worse, fail to discover) among fly-by-night precious-metals dealers. These are the tricks of the bucket-shop trade. Not all dealers use them, naturally, but they are far from uncommon.

1. Counterfeiting

Coins have been counterfeited almost as long as they have been minted. The Roman emperors were responsible for debasing their own coinage, and numerous cheats in the intervening centuries have followed their example. In Georgian times, for instance, it was a common practice (although a capital offense) to "sweat" coins by placing a number of them in a leather pouch and then vigorously shaking the pouch. The coins would rub against each other and leave a residue of gold dust in the pouch, which the "sweater" took as his profit. That's only one example among many illustrating the age-old popularity of debasing.

You don't have to worry about counterfeiting much if you are buying straight bullion. Bars or wafers from known refiners will be stamped to indicate their origins, and even those rare bars that are not so stamped can be readily enough assayed to determine their gold content. The same thing goes for bullion coins. It is the older, numismatic coins you really have to watch out for. So high are the premiums on numismatics that forgers make a profitable business out of fobbing off copies as originals.

A decade ago, numismatist Donald Hoppe identified dozens of commonly forged coins, some as old as the Byzantine era (a favorite period for forgers), others as recent as the twentieth century.[1] The situation has not improved since he wrote. Indeed, the 1970s surge in numismatic investing served not only to make rare coins all the more valuable, but gave notice to the counterfeiters that a whole new generation of coin-hungry marks was ready to be taken. Forgery of coins is as good a business today as it has ever been. The American Numismatic Association Certification Service reported only a few years back that about *one third* of all the coins it is asked to analyze eventually turn out to be fakes!

Most forgeries are made by taking a wax pressing of a rare coin and making a casting in metal from that mold. An expert caster can produce castings that are very nearly as sharp in detail as the original die-struck coin, and even though some of these castings can be identified as counterfeits with the jeweler's loupe, this is not always the case. Spotting a slightly "fuzzy" copy of an original is not a skill you can pick up quickly, and it is certainly not something to be left to the amateur. If you are beginning to invest in numismatics, have an expert give you a judgment on any dubious specimens before you buy.

The popular numismatic press frequently runs articles on forgeries, and reading such publications as *Coin World* can alert you to current scams, such as the recent Lebanese copies of old U.S. gold pieces. These were fairly easy to spot, since the casting process used in counterfeiting them left the details characteristically unclear, but many other copies are virtually indistinguishable from the originals. This is especially the case, as I've mentioned, with restrikes: they are not exactly forgeries, but the fine distinction will mean nothing to you if you end up paying a heavy premium for a restrike with no numismatic value.

If you are thinking of buying an apparent numismatic from a seller whose reputation is unclear, insist on a certificate of authenticity and on a guarantee of refund in case the coin turns out to be forged. And remember to beware of bargains. Anything being offered to you as a "steal" may end up being just that.

[1] See Hoppe, *How to Invest in Gold Coins.*

2. Assaying Tricks

Counterfeiting is a problem you may encounter when you are buying, not selling, your coins. When you are selling, on the other hand, you have to be careful of assaying, or weighing, tricks. You may go into a shop with a coin you believe to be "coin gold" (.900 fine) and have the dealer tell you it is only .850. You may hear that the ring you were sure was 18-Kt gold is "in fact" only 14-Kt or that the one-ounce medallion you want to sell actually weighs only nine tenths of an ounce. In all of these cases, you may be dealing with a buyer who makes a little extra profit illegally by "shaving" your weight before buying, and thus offering you less than full value.

The 1982 *Investors Guide*[2] to gold identifies four ways in which unscrupulous dealers manage to pay less for an item than it is actually worth:

- They simply give the customer a false weight, either by using dishonest scales or by using accurate scales and then translating the scale weight, with a false formula, into a light pennyweight equivalent.
- They misstate the gold content of an item, using as evidence an acid test that "proves" the coin you thought was coin gold is actually 30 percent copper.
- They fix the specific-gravity test, by which the density of the item is determined, and thus convince the customer that it is less pure than he thinks.
- They claim that a gold piece is merely gold-plated, and offer the customer a fraction of its actual value.

These are only the most common assaying tricks you may encounter as you try to sell gold. The major protection you have against them is to learn simple assaying yourself. You can purchase a nitric-acid testing kit or a specific-gravity kit in any large numismatic supply house and test your items yourself before you offer them for sale. That way, if there is a large discrepancy between your assessment and the potential buyer's, you will know that you are in the wrong shop.

You can also have your coin or bullion tested by an independent assayer. A list of reliable assayers is given on page 49. Unfortunately, the assay charges make this an unwise procedure unless a large amount of gold is involved. It makes no economic sense to pay a $50 assay fee on an item that will bring you only three times that in a shop. When you are uncertain as to the purity of an item, therefore, the smart course

[2] *Investors Guide: Gold Bullion and Coins.*

is to avoid the bucket shops and pay the slightly higher service charges you will encounter in a major dealer's business. That charge will amount to only a fraction of the money you could lose if you let an unknown dealer take you in.

Assayers

Ledoux & Co.
359 Alfred Avenue
Teaneck, N.J. 07666

Lucius Pitkin Inc.
50 Hudson Street
New York, N.Y. 10013

United States Assay Office
32 Old Slip
New York, N.Y. 10005

3. Price Juggling

Even if your dealer is scrupulous about stating the proper weight, you can still be taken in if he or she fails to quote you the correct daily spot price for gold on the day you want to sell. This is not as uncommon as you might think. The *Investors Guide* notes several methods by which less-than-honest dealers shave dollars off the spot price and thus get away with paying customers less than they deserve:

▪ They use the London and New York spot prices by turns, depending on which will give them an advantage. If gold is at $400 in New York and $405 in London, they buy at the New York rate and sell at the London. Switching prices like this, a dealer can sell an item immediately after buying it, at an unfair profit.

▪ They use spot prices from exchanges other than London and New York, to the same end.

▪ They use midday, rather than closing, prices, because these are difficult to verify and can afford them a profitable differential. An unscrupulous dealer, for example, can claim that his Telex machine has just noted a three-dollar drop in the spot price, and he must therefore pay you less than the figure you saw in the morning paper. Unless you actually see the Telex machine in evidence and he can show you the supposed drop, do not assume he is telling the truth.

▪ They claim that, for one reason or another, they cannot pay the spot price. "Refiners aren't paying it," they will tell you, or "Coins are being discounted now." All of this is nonsense. A reputable dealer makes his money on a reasonable commission, not by shaving the spot price.

Because such price juggling occurs with frequency among certain dealers, it is always a good idea for you to know, before you go in to sell an item, approximately what you should be paid for it. The day's spot price for gold is published in your paper every morning and broadcast on most morning news shows as well. Knowing the day's going rate, you can easily get a rough idea of how much a dealer should offer you, and then weigh this against his quote.

Say, for example, that you have a half-ounce nonnumismatic coin that you believe to be coin gold (.900 fine). That means that it contains 90 percent of a half ounce, or 45 percent of a full ounce, of pure gold. On its melt value alone, then, it ought to be worth 45 percent of the day's quoted price for gold. If you see by the paper that gold was $400 at the opening of the New York exchange, you will know that your coin is worth 45 percent of $400, or $180, melt value. Having that figure in mind when you go in to sell it, you can better determine what kind of deal you are getting. If the dealer offers you $170 or $175, he is taking a reasonable profit; if he suggests $125, you'll know you're in the wrong place. (If he offers you *more* than $180, you'd better reinspect both the coin and your figures: you might have a valuable numismatic piece and not even know it.)

Note that the price you'll be offered is generally going to be somewhat less than the price you yourself have calculated. You're never going to get the full $180, because the dealer has to make money too, and the way he does that is to charge you a fee. That fee, which is highly variable, is subtracted from the melt value of the item. This practice is entirely reasonable, but only if the fee itself is reasonable.

4. Dealers' Fees

We've already noted that assay and bar charges must be taken into consideration in any transaction involving straight bullion and that premiums on numismatic coins can be a major factor in the attractiveness of a given item in that market. Such "handling charges" are an inevitable part of the gold-trading world, and you should not be surprised when you are asked to pay them. You should, however, be careful that you don't pay so much in fees that you undercut the value of your investment.

What's a reasonable handling fee for gold transactions? There are no set, regulated fees, but there is a generally acceptable range. Bar charges I've already mentioned: expect to pay about 1 percent per ounce on the smaller, one-ounce bars and substantially less on the large ones. For bullion coins, the accepted premium charge is about 3 percent of the melt price; with gold at $400 an ounce, a one-ounce Maple Leaf therefore should cost you about $412.

In the case of numismatic coins, the range is much wider and more flexible. Depending partly on the coin itself, dealers will charge as little as 7 or 8 percent and as much as several hundred percent. In addition, you should know that there is always an accepted difference between the price at which you can sell a coin to a dealer and the price at which he will sell it to you. The dealer sells at an *ask price* and buys at a *bid price.* The difference between the two, which is called the *spread,* accounts for his margin of profit. The larger the spread, the more profit he is presumably making.

Spreads are common practice in any secondhand business, so you needn't feel cheated if Friendly Fred pays you $200 for a coin that he later resells for $225. As long as you are not paying an exorbitant fee for his trouble, his profit is not your concern. By "exorbitant," I mean above 4 or 5 percent on bullion coins and anything at all above what is listed in the pricing schedules on numismatics. Again you see the importance of acquainting yourself with the going rates before you shop.

5. Resale Problems

Because dealers' spreads are so varied, you should always find out, before you buy, what the dealer will be willing to give you for your item if you decide to resell it to him. The buy-back offer, of course, will not be an absolute figure, since value fluctuates with the spot price. What it should indicate is the percentage of premium over the spot price that you would be able to recoup on a resale. Ask the dealer before you buy to explain his or her other resale policies too: you need to know not only the spread, but also whether or not there is a waiting period before resale is permitted, what the guarantee of authenticity promises and what adjustment he will make if, through no fault of his own, a coin turns out to have been misrepresented.

These are the major problems you might encounter when you buy from the less well-known dealers. In addition, there are sometimes problems that arise *after* a transaction is made—chiefly problems of misrepresentation and failure to deliver. Ever since gold was opened up, in 1975, the Securities and Exchange Commission, which investigates fraud in commodities trading, has been deluged with complaints from people who have been bilked by dealers who seemed honest. The SEC, in response to these complaints, has brought numerous suits, charging firms with quite respectable-sounding names with misrepresenting their offers, using high-pressure sales tactics and failing to deliver on payment. Millions of dollars in advance payments are still being lost to these shady operators, and if you don't want to join the long list of their victims, I suggest that you thoroughly investigate any not-long-established firms before doing any business with them.

Your state attorney general's office can tell you what suits are pending against gold dealers in your area and whether or not your prospective buyer or seller is among those suspected of irregular practices. The Better Business Bureau and the SEC itself are other sources of information. Don't hesitate to check up on a firm before you give it your money. If there is any question about its good intentions or its financial stability, go to another firm; there is no shortage of them around.

Many people, eager to buy gold quickly, have given their money to shady firms and allowed the firm to hold the metal in exchange for a certificate. As I've pointed out, this is a common practice with reputable firms, but with an uncertain firm it can be very costly. Many of these trusting souls never see anything *but* the paper and are not aware that they have paid $350 an ounce for nonexistent metal. A good way to avoid that is to demand delivery upon payment. A better way is to refuse to deal with anyone whose reputation cannot be cleared by the Better Business Bureau, the state attorney general, the SEC or all three.

That may seem like a lot of trouble to go to just to clear a small coin sale, but I assure you it is worth it. If you don't believe me, you can ask the dozens of people who, in the past several years, have put down huge sums of money in exchange for worthless papers. Gold trading is hard enough when you're dealing with honest merchants. Why make it any more difficult by offering to play with the wolves?

The main risk is that you may pay good money for a "certificate" or a receipt that allegedly represents a specific amount of gold. Yet it is almost impossible for hundreds of newly formed gold dealers to make a legitimate profit through this system. Some claim they sell at spot prices and charge no transaction fees. They lure investors/speculators by spending millions on advertising. Behind the scenes, however, they are using the investors' money for their own private needs. After a few months or so, they fail for millions.

Such a practice was described on the front page of the New York *Times* on October 5, 1983. The suicide of Alan David Saxon, chairman of Gold Reserve of North America, set off a widespread investigation of the company's activities. It was found that Saxon, his wife and others closely related to the company had received $41,000,000 in personal loans from the company. This money came from investors who had been lured by the company's ads. The Attorney General of New York,

Robert Abrams, quoted the ads, which ran, "Come and buy gold and silver bullion, have a safe and secure investment, capitalize on the appreciation of these precious metals, and store them safely and securely in our own vaults in Utah."

As a result, the thirty to thirty-five thousand investors who thought they had $60,000,000 worth of gold in vaults had a scant one million. Not surprisingly, the company filed for bankruptcy. The "investors' " loss may well exceed $60,000,000.

During the summer of 1983, a New York State grand jury indicted two top executives of International Gold Bullion Exchange in Florida on charges of fraud and grand larceny. Investors in this company lost up to $40,000,000.

These are only two of the larger frauds uncovered in the past year; hundreds of smaller ones have also come to light.

RIDING THE GOLDEN TIGER

The gold market is frequently characterized as a field of unlimited opportunity—a magical, glittering arena where, with just a little luck, the small investor can make a king's ransom overnight. Gold trading is the Hollywood of the commodities world: it's the most glamorous, most intoxicating of all financial opportunities. Moreover, since gold was only $35 an ounce a decade ago and is now over ten times that, it seems all the more a field where quick fortunes are easy to come by. "If I invest my $2,000 now," the optimistic investor says, "it will turn into $20,000 before I know it."

It's true that fortunes have been made, and will continue to be made, in gold, but it's important to keep in mind also that opportunity can strike two ways. Gold went to over $800 in 1980, remember, and people who bought into the market at that price, confident it would continue to rise, are now ruefully licking their wounds. If you had bought just two ounces of gold at that price, you would by now have lost about a thousand dollars—not even counting inflation. The gold price continues to be volatile. Those of you who are considering buying into the market for speculative purposes—those of you who want to make a quick killing—should realize that gold *can* turn to lead as well as the other way around.

Assuming that you want to buy in, there are three basic questions you have to answer—questions that apply to your investment strategy no matter what form of gold (bullion, coins or futures) you have in mind. You have to ask yourself: 1) How much do I want to buy? 2) When do I want to buy it? 3) When do I want to sell it?

1) Determining how much you should buy is largely a function of how much in the way of liquid assets you have and how much risk capital you can afford to tie up in gold. The more you have to invest, needless to say, the wider your choice. The person with a spare $50,000 will probably want to consider splitting his or her gold investments among various related options, perhaps putting one third each in bullion, futures and coins. The person with only a thousand dollars to spend has a narrower choice: with that low an investment, the only reasonable options are bullion and bullion coins.

Whatever option you choose, however, you should keep that "risk capital" admonition in mind. No matter how "wide open" the gold market may be, you should not gamble more than a reasonable percentage of your worth (perhaps 10 or 15 percent) in this volatile market. Even if you are desperately eager to own gold, I still suggest that you split your investments, putting a small portion into bullion for starters and another portion into something less glamorous but more stable, such as the money markets. That way, you will be protected against inflation even if your "sure thing" in gold fails to pan out as expected.

There is just one rider to this rule, and that is, even if you have only limited capital, it still pays to buy in bulk. I don't advise you to enter the gold market by buying merely two or three wafers—I've already pointed out that bar charges can be your undoing there. It's better to save your money until you have enough to buy at least a one-ounce piece, such as a Maple Leaf or a Krugerrand.

2) The question of when to buy gold is not as easy as it may seem. The simple answer, of course, is to buy when the metal is low and sell when it is high. But say the spot price has been falling slowly for a couple of months. When do you know it's hit bottom? When do you buy in, confident that from here on in it's uphill? Or suppose the price has been rising. Do you buy in as quickly as possible, hoping that the upward trend will continue? Or do you wait for a slip, when others will be unloading gold more cheaply?

There are no pat answers to these questions, because gold, like any other commodity, is affected daily by supply and demand. In addition, there's the El Dorado Factor, which makes this particular commodity more volatile than nearly any other. Most analysts seem to agree, though, that it's better to get into the market when it is *steadily* climbing, rather than rapidly advancing—and that the worst time to get in, at least for the small investor, is in a period of radical fluctuation. The *Investors Guide* gives this advice:

Probably the best time to buy is when gold has been advancing steadily, though not dramatically, for at least two months—yet is far from its record high. . . . Small steady advances are usually followed by larger advances, more often than by declines. And even if a decline should occur, declines following steady advances are generally not of the panic variety. . . . One thing is certain. Whenever the price of gold . . . soars upward in a short period of time, it is going to come down again.

That has certainly been borne out by the events of the past couple of years.

How low will gold go? Assuming interest rates remain high, I'd say it could drop to as low as $200 an ounce. But you will probably be assured of a steady profit if you buy it even at $300 or $350 an ounce. To get that steady profit, though, you have to hold on to it for a while. This brings us to the trickiest of the three questions: when to get rid of what you have.

3) The most difficult, and ultimately the most crucial, question is when you should sell your holdings. Conventional wisdom might say that you should sell, and thus do your profit taking, as soon as the selling price is higher than the price you paid for it. This reasoning would be sound if it were not for two mitigating factors: dealers' fees and inflation. Dealers' fees and inflation are the one-two punch of gold dealing. If you fail to figure them in when you are considering unloading that hot property, you will be taking a beating, not a coup.

Suppose you have bought an amount of gold that, when you bought it, went for $3,000: with gold at $300 an ounce, that would be ten ounces of gold. You hold on to this purchase for, say, one full year—at which time the gold price rather suddenly jumps to $340 an ounce. What should you do? A simple look at the situation tells you you can now take in $3,400 for the $3,000 that you laid out. But is that really a good deal?

Not if you think of the one-two punch. Let's say you bought the gold in bullion form (the cheapest way) and paid a 5 percent "carrying charge" on it. That brings your initial investment up to $3,150. Then consider the inflation "charges." Supposing inflation was at 10 percent for the year since you bought the gold (not a radical supposition, considering recent history), the gold you bought at $3,000 now represents a $3,300 investment—that's the amount of current money you would need to cover the cost of what a year ago was only $3,000. So, with charges and inflation combined, the real cost of your gold is now $3,450. If you decide to sell it, therefore, at the $340 figure, you will not have gained $400 at all. You will have lost $50.

In today's economy, it is very unlikely that inflation will drop drastically over the long run. Therefore, you should always calculate, whenever you are considering making a big kill, whether or not the money you take in per ounce has kept pace with the falling value of money. Gold is a fine investment *over time,* but it can be a poor one in the short term. Getting rid of an "unprofitable" gold buy after a year or two may prove in the end to be a less sensible idea than holding on to it until, eventually, it overtakes inflation.

History suggests that gold prices do eventually overtake inflation, and if you have the patience to wait until they do, you may ultimately realize good profits. To do so, however, you have to be willing to wait: to forgo taking quick gains in the expectation of bigger ones. Fortunes are made in gold, but not too many of them are built on quick profit taking. Those who do well over time understand that fact.

You have probably all heard the limerick that bemoans the fate of the "lady from Niger"—the one who rode on the back of a tiger and ended up inside it. Your problem, as a small gold investor, is to avoid a similar fate. You have to ride the "tiger" of golden opportunities without getting turned into a victim of the very possibilities you find so exciting. The gold market, no less than the back of a tiger, is an uncertain as well as exciting place to find yourself. If you "ride" the market with that in mind, you can come out at least solvent, and possibly rich. If you insist on playing the market for all it's worth—insist on baiting the tiger for a better ride—you may end up, like the hapless lady, inside, rather than on top of, the game.

PART **II**

THE PEOPLE'S CHOICE

CHAPTER 4

THE POOR MAN'S GOLD

If gold has been traditionally associated with royalty and riches, silver has been seen as its exceedingly poorer cousin, a kind of consolation metal which greedy kings and princes would take only if they couldn't get gold. Among the medieval alchemists, gold was a symbol of the sun and silver a symbol of the moon—the implication being that the white metal could boast only a reflected glory. In modern times, this condescension toward silver has continued, and more than one writer has paid it the grudging compliment of calling it "the poor man's gold." Considering the beauty and utility of silver, this is a little hard to understand. But then, as we saw in Chapter 1, people's reactions to precious metals are not always governed by good sense.

There is at least one sound reason for valuing silver less highly than gold, and that is its relative abundance. Silver is a very rare metal—occurring in only about one part per hundred million of the earth's crust—but it is not nearly as rare as gold: gold occurs in about only one tenth of that amount. Obviously this partly accounts for the difference in the metals' reputations.

But as we shall see in a moment, silver as compared to gold is an infinitely more useful metal, and you might expect that its utility would go a long way to overcoming the gap between the metals' prices. This is not the case. Throughout history, gold has been overpriced and silver has been underpriced, and this is far more clearly the case today, when silver supplies are diminishing at the same time that new industrial uses are being found for the metal each day.

What does this mean to you, the small investor?

Basically, it's very good news. Because silver lacks the emotional appeal of gold, it continues to command a lower price relative to gold than its utility alone might dictate. Even the Hunt brothers' recent finagling of the silver futures market failed to boost its price significantly upward for more than a few dizzy months. As of this writing, gold is selling for $350 to $400 an ounce and silver is $7.50 to $10. That's a ratio of more than 40 to 1 between two of the world's most highly respected investments. A good deal of the disparity is the result of the late-1970s gold speculation, but traditionally the ratio has always been unreasonably high, and the current ratio is really only an illogical extension of the "norm."

For the small investor or speculator, this means that getting into the precious-metals market in silver is a great deal easier and less expensive (and always has been) than getting into it with gold. Today, as at many critical moments in history, silver is the "people's choice." Calling it the poor man's gold might be taken as an insult, but it can also be seen as a mark in its favor. If you are not a modern-day prince, this "lesser" metal might be exactly what you are looking for.

If you are interested in holding silver, you are part of a long and fascinating story, for throughout human history this metal has played just as critical a role in economics as gold. You could even say that its role was more important—or at least more evident—because while few people in the past ever got to handle gold, millions of common folk had access to the "people's choice."

THE PEOPLE'S CHOICE: A BRIEF HISTORY

Silver has been known since the Bronze Age (4000–1000 B.C.), and as early as that misty time it was being used as a medium of exchange.[1] Silver artifacts have been found in the tombs of the Egyptian pharaohs dating from about 3000 B.C., and it is likely—though not provable—that silver was being mined and worked long before that.

By that era, too, silver and gold were already recognized as being in some way related, and the first recorded ratio of value between them was set down in the legal code of the first great Egyptian pharaoh, Menes. It stipulated that one part of gold was equal in value to two and a half parts of silver. Apparently the ancient Egyptians, in spite of their reverence for the sun, had not yet acquired that equivalent reverence for the "sun's metal" that has tended to make subsequent ratios so much higher. If the 1 to 2½ ratio were observed today, of course, silver would be selling at $175 an ounce—something that even the Hunts never dreamed of.

After they discovered how to smelt and refine silver, the first uses the ancients put it to were probably decorative: they used the highly malleable metal to make such items as jewelry and fancy tableware. There is some evidence, however, that as smelting techniques improved, more "utilitarian" objects were also made. In the Roman Republic and in

[1] Much of the information in the following section is taken from Marc Hudgeons's fine *Official Investors Guide to Buying and Selling Gold, Silver and Diamonds.*

ancient Athens, military equipment (swords, shields and breastplates) were sometimes made of silver.

But the most significant change in the use of the metal came when it was discovered that silver could be made into coins. Some ancient peoples used flat silver pieces as a medium of exchange even before coinage came in, and hoarding these silver "slugs" was a kind of primitive banking system. When ancient rulers began to mint coins, this hoarding process increased, for with the image of a ruler on a silver coin, a poor farmer would have not only an attractive, patriotic memento, but a widely accepted medium of exchange.

It is thought that government minting began in ancient Lydia around 800 B.C. The Lydians favored gold, but silver soon began to be used as well, and when silver coins started to circulate—the Babylonians were the first to mint them—the human race was introduced to the fascinating and frequently turbulent world of conflicting money standards, or bimetallism.

This book is not the place to review the many arguments pro and con for a double-metal money standard. I just want to point out that the introduction of silver coinage was one of the most significant events in monetary history, because it made available for the first time a durable standard of value that was not the exclusive property of wealthy merchants and rulers. Silver was a standard metal for coins from late antiquity into the twentieth century, and throughout that long span of time, whatever the legal or local fortunes of bimetallism, it was silver that most people hoarded.

In the United States, silver was adopted as a standard of value back in 1792, when the nation's first mint was established. Gold, however, was also accepted as a standard, and from 1792 until 1900 the country was on a bimetallic standard. This created serious problems throughout our country's history.

The major problem was the inability of the government minting system to maintain a fixed and workable ratio of value between the two metals. In 1792, when bimetallism was established, the Secretary of the Treasury, Alexander Hamilton, suggested that 1 : 15 be set up as the mint's "official" ratio of gold to silver value. He based this suggestion on the current market ratio between the two metals. This made sense to the Congress, and they went along with his plan.

The trouble was that the free-market ratio, unlike the mint's set ratio, was constantly changing in response to market forces and the official ratios of other governments. As long as the market ratio stayed at 1 : 15, everything was fine. But it didn't stay there very long, and when it started to fluctuate, one or another of the metal standards was always in danger of being melted down for bullion, rather than being returned to the mint. Naturally this wreaked havoc on the relative prices of the metals, and on the system in general.

What was happening—and it happened throughout the nineteenth century—was that old economist's nightmare Gresham's law. This law —named after Elizabeth I's master of the mint, Thomas Gresham— states that in a bimetallic system, "bad money drives out good." That is, when you have two standards of value operating at a fixed government ratio, the metal with the higher value in the free market is "driven out" of circulation by the weaker metal, simply because when people have a choice between holding on to a "good" coin or a "bad" one, they will spend the bad one and hoard the good.

It's the disparity between the fixed government ratio and the floating world market prices that causes Gresham's law to operate. Say the U.S. gold-to-silver ratio is 1 : 15, as it was in 1792, but the floating world ratio is 1 : 16. That is, the "official" value of gold is less than the price you can get for it on the free market. What do you do, in this situation, with your gold and silver coins?

The government would like you to trade them both with equal facility, just as if its official ratio were the only working ratio. But that's not what people do. If you see the possibility of capitalizing on the ratio disparity, what you do is this.

First, you take your silver coins (let's say, to make the example easier to follow, that you have 15 ounces of them) to the government mint, where you exchange them for gold coins. In a 1 : 15 bimetallic system, this means that the government will give you one ounce of gold. You take that ounce of gold and sell it on the free market as bullion, receiving more silver coins in payment. But since the free market ratio is 1 : 16, you get not fifteen, but sixteen, ounces of silver coins for that ounce of gold—even though you have just bought it for fifteen. That leaves you with one ounce of silver as a profit. You pocket this profit, return to the government mint with your remaining fifteen ounces of silver and repeat the process.

After a few of these trading trips, you will have amassed a very nice profit in silver. But what has happened to the gold? It has been "driven out" of circulation into private bullion hoards, and is therefore lost to the government, whose gold supplies, because of your transactions, are gradually being depleted.

This happened periodically throughout the nineteenth century, with gold disappearing at certain times and silver at others, depending on whether the bimetallic market ratio was higher or lower than the mint's. It was an extremely fluid, but unstable, system. The government tried to regulate it periodically by restricting or increasing the amount of metal it would issue, but these attempts did nothing to eliminate the underlying confusions of bimetallism, and through much of the late-nineteenth century the story of silver was the story of the conflict between those who wanted the price of the metal to be artificially hiked up by the government and those who wanted "cheap" silver to continue functioning as the "people's" metal.

The high-water mark of the conflict was the presidential election of 1896, during which the flamboyant Populist candidate William Jennings Bryan gave his famous cross-of-gold speech, denouncing those who wanted to limit the free coinage of silver. Bryan, who was a champion of western farmers and miners, favored this all-stops-out bimetallism, according to Douglas Casey, because he knew that, with silver as well as gold backing the dollar, it would simply be easier to print more money.[2] His real goal was inflation: a system of cheap, ready money that would favor his constituents by driving up prices for their goods.

Bryan lost, but that did not really end the turmoil about silver. Silver continued to be a nettlesome issue, for Populists and "sound money" advocates alike, deep into the twentieth century, with the government using its own buying and selling power to continue to modify the price, just as it had before 1896. At the same time, silver continued to "back" the dollar, just as gold had earlier. It wasn't until the 1960s that the government finally demonetized silver—that is, recognized that its market price no longer bore any relation to the paper money that supposedly represented it. In 1964, as a final signal of this recognition, the Treasury stopped making silver coins; it switched over to "clad" coins composed of copper covered with nickel.

I have given you this sketchy overview of silver coinage because it is important for you, as a small investor, to understand how closely silver has been linked to government activity in the past—and to realize that it could always be so linked again. As long as silver is kept in any government hoards (and the U.S. Government has about 140 million ounces of silver stockpiled in the strategic reserve right now in addition to the 32,800,000 ounces in the Treasury), decisions in Washington can affect the price and fluidity of your silver. Indeed, as we will see in a moment, manipulation of federal stockpiles is a principal factor affecting the price of silver today. Just because the metal is no longer monetized does not mean that Washington (not to mention London, Moscow, Johannesburg, etc.) does not have an influence on its value.

But in the twentieth century, government regulation of silver prices is

[2] See Casey, *Crisis Investing*, p. 188.

a little less momentous than it used to be. This is because silver is no longer valued chiefly as a medium of exchange: today it is less a symbol, and much more clearly a commodity. A good deal of silver does still go into coins, but a far greater proportion is taken up by various industries.

INDUSTRY'S DARLING

I said in Chapter 1 that, although gold does possess certain properties that make it attractive to industry, its value does not reside chiefly in its practical applicability. This is not the case with silver. Even if silver were no longer widely employed in coins and medallions, its value would still be immense. This, you will recall, is why I said that silver is undervalued relative to gold: if silver were measured on its uses alone, it would be far *more* valuable than gold.

Silver has always been a useful metal, even before this highly industrialized century. Because of its malleability and reflectiveness, it has always been popular with jewelers, and these qualities are no less important today, both to jewelers and to manufacturers of coins. But, compared to its other qualities, these "aesthetic" advantages have gradually become less significant. Especially since World War II, the utility of the white metal has become much more highly prized than its beauty.

To give you a quick idea of how silver's application has changed since the war, let me quote a few figures from Roy Jastram's fascinating study *Silver: The Restless Metal.* Speaking of "silver's industrial revolution," Jastram traces the comparative uses of silver in coinage and in industry from 1949 to 1971. In 1949, of the 216 million ounces of silver consumed worldwide, 84 million ounces, or about 39 percent, went into coins. The remaining 132 million ounces, or 61 percent, went to industry. Even then, you can see, silver had already become industry's darling.

But by 1971, after the United States had stopped minting silver coins, this imbalance was even clearer. In that year, of the 415 million ounces consumed, less than 7 percent went to coins. The remaining 93 percent —387 million ounces—found its way into industrial applications.

This trend has continued into the 1980s. According to U.S. Bureau of Mines figures quoted by Jastram, of the 165 million ounces of silver consumed in the United States in 1979 (the United States remains the world's largest consumer of silver), only 2.6 million ounces were used in coins, medallions and other commemorative objects. The rest went into industry.

But what industry? Which industries are the major users of silver, and what does that mean to you as a potential purchaser of the metal?

By far the largest user of silver is the photographic industry, with Eastman Kodak accounting for the consumption of more silver per year than any other single firm. Since the early days of photography, in the mid-nineteenth century, silver, because of its peculiar sensitivity to light, has been a major ingredient in film. With the boom that photography has been enjoying since about 1970, silver will no doubt continue to be channeled first and foremost into film.

No attempt to find a reliable substitute for silver in film has been successful so far. Only a few years ago, Wallace Hanson, of the editorial staff of *Popular Photography,* dismissed the idea of a substitute being found in the near future as extremely remote.[3] So the chances are strong that silver will continue to be essential to this vast industry—an industry that, in 1979, used 65 million ounces of the metal. That was almost 40 percent of the total consumed in the United States.

After photography comes electronics. Because of its fine conductivity, silver is widely used in this field, principally in contacts and conductors. Batteries also use silver, and if you add these uses together, you find that in 1979 about 24 percent of the silver consumed—42 million ounces—went into electronics. A not insignificant portion of this now goes into transistors and home video hardware—and you know how rapidly that field is expanding.

After photography and electronics, which together account for almost two thirds of U.S. consumption, come a string of critical but less expansive fields. The major secondary uses of silver are in sterling ware, electroplated ware, chemical catalysis, alloys, solders and jewelry. Then come minor amounts used in bearings, mirrors and medical and dental applications: one of the most interesting features of the metal is that it is fatal to certain bacteria, and this accounts for some of its value to medicine.

And this may be only a beginning. The Industrial Revolution transformed the metal from primarily a monetary and decorative item to an industrial one. There is no way of telling yet what new uses for silver we will find as the Space Age and the industry-rich Computer Age proceed. Douglas Casey notes that over three hundred new uses for silver were found in 1978 alone.[4] With that kind of past performance, silver's continuing industrial value seems assured. As a result, the metal remains a very attractive option for those with limited capital.

[3] See his "Is Silver Essential in Photography?" in Louis Carabini, ed. *Everything You Need to Know Now About Gold and Silver.*
[4] Casey, op. cit., p. 196.

But there are other reasons for supposing that silver will remain a sound buy. Its enormous value to industry is only one element of its attractiveness. To understand why silver buyers are often so confident about their investments, you have to appreciate not only the continuing demand for its use, but also the worldwide supply. Fortunately for the investor, that supply has been diminishing for some years and is likely to continue doing so.

THE CONSUMPTION-PRODUCTION SHORTFALL

For many years, one of the happy facts about the silver market has been that production consistently lags behind consumption. This fact does not delight everybody: it's not welcome news to the jeweler who has more orders than he has silver to fill them. But to you, as a novice investor, it is very good news indeed.

The shortfall between production and consumption varies slightly from time to time, but the *fact* of the continuing lag has been obvious for years. Throughout the 1970s, that lag ran at an average of well over a hundred million ounces a year.[5] In 1976, for example, as all those Bicentennial medallions were being produced, the total world production of silver—from newly mined ores plus salvage—amounted to 323 million ounces, while the total consumption was 430 million ounces—a shortfall of 107 million ounces. This was not an atypical year, and obviously when you're dealing with a supply-demand lag of that dimension, the price is at worst going to stay fairly steady, and at best be gradually rising. As Harry Browne puts it, "Silver is in a long-term bull market, caused by an imbalance between consumption and production."[6]

There are good reasons why this shortfall situation is unlikely to change in the near future, and why a small investor can more or less bank on this bullish trend being constant.

The first reason is that, while consumption/demand goes up every time a new use for silver is found, the amount of silver that can profitably be mined to meet this need is relatively constant—or rather, constantly diminishing. Most of the big old mines have pretty well played themselves out, and it is not very probable that new ones are going to be discovered.

This is because silver was laid down in the earth's crust millions of

⁵ The figures in this section are taken from Handy & Harman estimates as reported in Harry Browne's *New Profits from the Monetary Crisis,* p. 271.
⁶ Ibid., p. 291.

years ago by a process that geologists call "epithermal deposition." That's a fancy way of saying that the veins in which silver are found tended, when they were molten, to congeal more richly (more densely) near the surface of the earth than they did deep down. As a result of this type of deposition, most of the world's richest veins are located at or near the planet's surface.

The deeper you go into a silver mine, therefore, the poorer the ore you extract. That is, the more base metal (usually lead, copper or zinc) you find mixed in with the more precious silver. So the deeper you go, the less profitable it is to mine silver. Because of this economic fact, many of the world's silver mines are close to being played out: it just doesn't pay to dig deeper.

But there is another factor to consider: Virtually all of the silver mined today, no matter how close to the surface it is, is found along with baser metals. Over two thirds of the silver being produced today is mined as a *by-product* of these baser metals, and surveys of potential future veins indicate that about 90 percent of the silver there is found in this same "impure" state. On average, a mine will yield 20 ounces of silver per *ton* of base metal!

What this means for the supply factor is that silver is *inelastic* in response to price. If silver were mined by and for itself, and there were still a good supply available, you would expect that when the market price went up, production would increase to meet the rising demand— and thus bring the price down. Production, that is, would be *elastic* in response to price rises. But this is not the case with silver. No matter how high the price goes (unless it's astronomical), it still does not pay a producer to radically increase his mining. This is so for two reasons.

First, there is simply not enough silver in current veins to make the extra production and labor costs worthwhile. And second, when a producer mines new silver, he is also mining new lead, copper or zinc. Since these base metals, not the silver, are often his principal products, he would be taking the chance of overmining them, thus depressing *their* prices, just so he could make a quick profit on his by-product. It just isn't worth the gamble, and that is one reason that silver comes out of the ground so slowly—one reason, in other words, that supply remains inelastic.

But inelastic supply is only half the story—only half the reason that silver is likely to remain a solid investment. The other half of the story is that the silver which is used in industry, although it is an absolutely essential component of industrial processes, is used in such small quantities compared to the overall manufacturing cost that, even if the metal's price skyrocketed, the demand would be very little diminished. In

economic terms, this means that *demand is also inelastic:* it responds
slowly, if at all, to price changes.

To understand why this is so, let's assume you are a manufacturer of
transistor radios and that you use silver in each of your products to
make the electrical connections. You don't use very much silver—most
of your raw material is plastic—but the small amount you do use is
essential.

Say a radio costs you ten dollars to manufacture and that the price of
the silver you use in it is 50 cents. What would happen to your demand
for silver—how much more or less firmly would you want it—if the
metal suddenly jumped 100 percent in cost? Would you continue to buy
silver if it doubled in price overnight?

Yes, you would. The 50 cents' worth of silver you had been using
would now be worth a dollar, so you would have to spend 50 cents
more on each radio for raw materials. But that 50 cents would represent
only a 5 percent increase on the total cost of each radio, and you could
easily pass such an increase on to your customers. Because the amount
of silver you used was small to begin with, your demand could remain
pretty constant—in other words, inelastic—unless the price really went
through the roof.

This is exactly what happens all the time in the industries that use
silver. They continue to buy the metal at almost any price, because it is
needed and because that price is only one factor in the overall cost of
production. Douglas Casey sums it up nicely: "Eastman-Kodak will not
stop making film, IBM stop making computers, nor the U.S. Navy stop
making submarines just because the price of one small—but essential—
component rises."[7]

Since both supply and demand are inelastic, silver should be a
surefire investment. The only thing that puts a fly in the ointment is that
the price can always be deflated by the actions of major holders, most of
whom are governments. This is not disastrous, but as a potential silver
buyer you should be aware of these holders' presence. Their decisions
are continually affecting the worldwide price of silver, and if you are
going to purchase silver wisely, you have to take these decisions into
account.

I've painted a pretty rosy picture of silver's future, and I believe it's
an accurate one. But the actions of governments and major investors—
not to mention such speculators as the Hunts—can always upset the
applecart, and for this reason there are no more guarantees in silver
than there are in gold.

7 Casey, op. cit., p. 193.

NO GUARANTEES

Can the price go down? Sure it can. It has gone down in the past, and it undoubtedly will again. Although the silver market is not nearly as risky as the gold market, you can still walk into trouble if you believe that, because both supply and demand are inelastic, you have nothing to worry about.

The main depressants on the silver price come from the major holders of the metal, both government and private. The way they get the price down is to sell some of their holdings. This makes more silver available, and consequently the price falls.

This is important for two reasons: First, by "flooding" the market with their stockpiled silver, the major holders regulate the market, thus preventing both the "corner" that the Hunts almost achieved and the kind of "soar/crash" syndrome that is every investor's nightmare. Second, the unloading of stockpiled silver helps to make up for the shortfall, which, as we've seen, is a constant factor in the market.

If it weren't for periodic government dishoarding, that shortfall might have already led to serious economic problems. In that 1976 shortfall of 107 million ounces, for example, the deficit was made up by a variety of major holders' dishoarding. To satisfy demand and also to keep down prices, the U.S. Government sold 8.3 million ounces of silver. Private investors, who frequently dishoard even more than the government, got rid of 35 million ounces. And (here is the surprising part) another 63 million ounces were sold from silver exported (legally and illegally) from India.

India is the uncertain factor in the silver market, and that has been the case for many years. Indian industry uses a fair amount of the metal, but that is not the significant factor. What is crucial is that hoarding is traditional and widespread in that poor country: many people literally wear their bank accounts on their persons, in the form of silver bracelets and other jewelry. In addition, wealthier Indians—and the government itself—hold an unknown amount of silver. It has been estimated by one industry expert that there are now over 300 million ounces of silver being held in India.

This is a large "stockpile," of course, and the difficulty of predicting the future price of silver is largely a result of the fact that we don't know for sure how much of this silver, and of the silver in other stockpiles, will be put on the market, or at what rate this will happen. India has the capacity, probably, to cover most of the world's deficit for some years to come, but whether or not it will do so—and at what rate—is still an economic mystery.

One thing is certain: the total availability of silver is falling, and it will continue to fall. Nobody knows the exact size of world silver stockpiles, Indian or otherwise, but it is generally acknowledged that, however large they are, they are inexorably getting smaller. Also, silver is not always recoverable from the many industrial processes in which it is used. It's a more reactive element than gold, and so in many cases, after it is used, it is not recoverable. In addition, a lot of it goes into products —transistor radios and computers, for example—in which it becomes a stable, working part of the item. And of course even if it's made into jewelry, it may stay in that form forever. The upshot of all this is that we are "losing" silver each year.

Recovery operations have increased as the price of silver has risen, since it becomes more profitable to salvage silver (from used film, for example) as the market price rises. As a result, a good deal of the silver that used to be thrown away is now being salvaged and recycled. But even with a very efficient system of salvaging, and even with the gradual unloading of stockpiles, the consumption-production lag still exists. We are gradually running out of silver.

The answer to where the silver price will go—and to the related question of whether it's still a good investment—depends, therefore, on how big you think the world stockpiles are, and on how fast you think they will diminish. Your guess is as good as mine on this score, though most experts seem to agree that, while silver may not be as glamorous or as intriguing a "get rich quick" market as gold, it's a pretty solid bet for the novice.

Now that the price has come down from the ludicrous heights it was pushed to by the Hunts, investing in silver should remain a relatively safe venture for some time. There are factors that could depress the market, and I'll go into them a little more in Chapter 6. But if things go along as they have been going, silver should remain fairly sound. There are no guarantees, naturally, but if you're going to invest in precious metals, silver seems a sensible choice. And it has the great advantage— aside from its bullish market—of being far more affordable (in terms of bulk per dollar) than gold. That, as we'll see now, is only one of its advantages.

CHAPTER 5

SILVER: YOUR OPTIONS

When most people think of silver, they usually have in mind not the ore that is extracted from the ground or the silver that goes into coins, but the shiny "sterling" silver that is used to manufacture silver plate or silverware. Even those of us who do not own a silver tea service ourselves have seen such services in other people's homes or in museums, and for most of us it is this manufactured form of the metal which seems the most common form of silver.

Because many brides still pick out their silver patterns as part of the rigmarole of their weddings, and because silver tea services and sugar bowls and platters are still fairly common in American homes, it is important to point out that, although "sterling" silver of this sort is indeed a common and fairly high-grade type of silver, it is by no means the only type—and in fact, for purposes of investment, it is not the most desirable.

For purposes of investment, that glittering silver service that has been the pride and joy of your family for three generations may be worth very little. Its bullion content—the portion of its total weight which is pure, or bullion, silver—may be so small that selling it as scrap silver may be a mistake. In the rush to unload family antiques that occurred a couple of years ago, many people sold such heirlooms at a substantial loss, because they were taken in by unscrupulous dealers who severely "underestimated" the amount of melt-silver content.

If these people had been aware that not all silver is the same—if they had been acquainted with some of the basic grades of this popular precious metal—they might have made out better in their transactions. That's one of the reasons for this chapter and the following one. I want to make you aware that when you are dealing in silver, no less than when you are dealing in gold, you have to know not only *that* an item is silver, but also *what kind* of silver it is and how much of its value is intrinsic, as opposed to extrinsic—or imagined.

Silver, just like gold, must be assessed in terms both of the quantity you are buying or selling and in terms of the quality of the metal itself. In the chapter on your options in gold, I spoke about fineness and karats, about troy ounces and pennyweights and melt value. Except for karats, all these terms apply to silver too, but in addition there are a few terms peculiar to the white metal.

SILVER: BASIC TERMS

To many of the uninitiated, "sterling" represents the quintessence of silver, the highest imaginable grade. Some people even suppose that sterling is "pure," or 100 percent, silver. Supposing this, as we'll see, could get you into serious financial trouble, because while sterling is a quite reputable grade of manufactured silver, it is far from being pure.

The purity, or fineness, of silver is measured in the same way that purity is measured in reference to gold: in terms of proportion of the precious metal to the weight of the item in which that metal is contained. Just as in the case of gold, an item which is absolutely pure silver would be designated "1.000 fine silver." But, as we've already seen, it is virtually impossible to refine a manufactured item—whether it's a coin, a ring or a bar of bullion—to that degree of fineness, and so for legal purposes any item that is thought to be "completely" pure is stamped ".9995 silver" instead. The assumption here is that a tiny fraction of alloy remains, but that for all practical purposes the item is totally silver.

Just as .9995 gold is the highest grade of gold you can buy, so .999 silver is the highest of its kind. If you're thinking of buying silver purely as an investment medium, this is the quality of silver you want, ideally. And if you purchase silver in bullion form from one of the major assayers or banks, this "pure" silver is what you will get. A ten-ounce bar of .999 fine silver (sometimes the refinery goes one step further and identifies it as .999+ fine) from Engelhard or Johnson Mathey will contain, theoretically, exactly ten ounces of pure metal—and it will be sold for exactly ten times the current spot price per ounce of silver, plus a small premium.

But supposing you are not buying bullion? Supposing you are looking at a coin, or one of those silver services? The grade of such items varies, but one thing is fairly constant. Nothing aside from bullion (and a few very old manufactured items) is made from .999 silver. Silver of this purity is simply too soft to be practical, and so silversmiths, whether they are minting coins or chasing teapot spouts, virtually always alloy their silver with copper or zinc, so that it will fulfill its intended use. Contrary to popular belief, there is no such thing as a "solid silver" table setting around today—unless it was made several centuries ago and has somehow escaped being melted down in the interim.

Items that are *said* to be solid silver can contain anywhere from a small portion of alloy to a very small portion of silver, so the buyer has to be very careful when purchasing "silver" items. Because the alloy in a silver item is worthless in terms of melt value, you have to know, before you buy, just how much alloy you are getting. In other words, you have to know just how fine the piece is. That's why stamps and hallmarks are so important on old silver—although, as we'll see, they are no guarantee that you are getting what you pay for. Hallmarks can be forged—which is why it is important for you to know, before you get ready to buy, the official silver percentages of the most popular grades. These are a bit more clearly identified than in the case of gold.

The percentage of alloy to silver can of course be almost anything in a worked piece, but there are three silver-to-alloy combinations that are among the most common. If you are shopping for worked silver and not silver bullion, these are the grades you will run into most often:

1. Sterling

Sterling, the most commonly known of major silver grades, is also the oldest officially recognized one. The designation "sterling" dates from an English statute of 1343, in which the first two letters of the word "Easterling" were dropped to make the new term "sterling." This term was then subsequently applied to all silver which had been or was being made by the Easterlings, a German immigrant band that produced much of the English silver at the time. "Sterling" silver, in other words, is the descendant of that silver which was first made by medieval Germans in the East of England.[1]

Although today the term is applied indiscriminately to silver of a variety of grades, it actually has a very precise definition. Sterling silver, according to professional silversmiths, is silver that is at least .925 fine —that is, which contains no more than seventy-five parts per thousand of alloy. This is pretty pure silver, and it is generally considered the finest grade that can be easily shaped and will wear well. That is why it is so common.

Sterling silver, although it originated in England, is now found worldwide, from Asia to the New World. Certain hallmarks are traditionally identified as sterling marks even if the word sterling does not appear on the piece, and you can also be sure that you have real sterling

[1] See Seymour Wyler, *The Book of Old Silver.* Information in this section was also drawn from Marc Hudgeons, op. cit.

silver if the pieces you are considering are stamped with the numbers 925, .925 or 925/1000. Assuming, of course, that they are not forged.

2. Britannia Silver

A higher grade of silver than sterling, Britannia silver is the finest silver used in manufacturing, although, because of its softness, its uses are limited: you will seldom find pieces other than flatware stamped "Britannia." Its percentage designation is .958 or .9584, meaning that only a little more than 4 percent of its content is alloy.

Britannia, which is commonly stamped with the figure of the culture heroine Britannia (a kind of British Statue of Liberty), was first designated an official grade of silver back in 1696. At that time, coins were frequently melted down to be used as silverware; to stop this debasement, the British Government shrewdly made the permissible quality of noncoin silver higher than that for coin silver. This made it uneconomical for people to melt down their coins (since refining out the silver in them would be too expensive to make the process worthwhile) and gave future collectors one of their most valued, and rare, grades of the metal.

3. Coin Silver

The third common grade of silver you may find is known as coin silver; like coin gold, it is .900 fine. This means that in a piece of coin silver, one tenth of the material is alloy and nine tenths is silver. As the name implies, this is a common grade of silver for coins—or rather, was, before modern coins began being made of copper and nickel. Coin silver is still commonly used in the many commemorative medallions that have flooded the market in recent years.

It is an interesting note that manufacturers of silver wares are often very fond of coin silver, because to obtain it, all they have to do is melt down or reshape old .900 coins; there's no need to refine out the pure silver and then realloy it, since the exact silver content of the original coin is known and the new object (which can be sold at more than the melt value, since it is manufactured) can simply be stamped "coin silver." Coin silver is sufficiently attractive for many worked pieces, and because it does not require mixing with an alloy, it's much easier to use than sterling or Britannia.

Sterling, Britannia and coin silver are the three high grades you are most likely to come across as you shop for silver wares, but they hardly exhaust the field. Silver can of course be alloyed in almost any combination, and as we'll see later on, this can lead to problems. If you stick with these three grades—and deal only with a known, reliable dealer— you should avoid most of those problems.

But remember, as with gold, that when you purchase silver, unless you are purchasing it as an antique or a collectible (this includes numismatic coins), the silver that you are buying is not equivalent to the total weight of the item in question, but only to the percentage of that weight that is indicated by the grade name. That's why buying .999 bullion is basically an easier task than shopping around for Britannia. When you buy .999 fine silver, you know that for every ounce of weight you purchase, you're getting one ounce of silver at near market, or spot, prices.

When you buy less-than-pure silver, this is not the case. A one-ounce piece of sterling, when silver is selling at $10 an ounce, is not worth ten dollars to melt. It is worth only 92.5 percent of that price, or about $9.25. If the one-ounce piece is made of coin silver, it's worth only 90 percent of the spot price, or $9. Even if you're going to be buying silver in such low quantities as this, it's important for you to remember that, in terms of bullion or melt value, the "silver" item you purchase must always be discounted by the price of its alloy and by the refining cost.

As I've noted, this is true for all silver except .999 fine silver. Since that is the highest grade of the metal, and is thus the easiest to buy, let's look at your silver options by considering this "pure" silver first.

OPTION 1: SILVER BULLION

As with gold, the cheapest and most direct way of owning silver is to buy silver bullion wafers or bars. When you buy silver bullion from a recognized refinery or a bank that deals with such a refinery, you are assured of getting nearly pure silver at or near the day's spot price for the metal. If you purchase a one-ounce wafer of the metal when silver is $10 an ounce, you will—or should—pay no more than about $11 for it. A 1,000-ounce bar would cost $10,000, which would be actual spot, or market, price, plus a commission of about 1 percent or less. That is a much smaller commission than you would expect to pay for silver in any other form.

The advantages of owning silver in bullion form are identical to those of owning gold in this form. In a bar or wafer, the metal is compact, portable, inexpensive and pure. In addition, since silver is so much cheaper per ounce than gold, the same outlay of investment will give you a considerably larger store of physical metal when you buy silver than when you buy gold. I mentioned that you can easily hold $5,000 worth of gold (with gold at about $500 an ounce) in the palm of your hand. The same value in silver takes up very much more space—so much so, in fact, that if you bought this much silver, you would want to consider a bank safety-deposit box or a safe in your home. Here, too, the same information applies as for gold: when you choose actually to hold your investment physically, you should be sure to take out the appropriate insurance policies and follow reasonable storage precautions.

The option of allowing the bank or dealer to keep your physical silver for you also involves the same precautions as in the case of gold. When you don't accept delivery of the metal yourself, you must be sure that you do receive a certificate for it, showing the weight and fineness of the purchase as well as its identifying bar number or numbers. All bullion purchases sold by reputable firms (Engelhard, Handy & Harman, Johnson Mathey, etc.) are stamped with the firm's own hallmark and with these other identifying figures; do not buy silver that does not have them, because even if your pig in a poke turns out to be .999 fine, you will still have to pay assaying charges to determine that. When a bar is stamped by a recognized refiner, you already know what it contains, and it is readily marketable. (See the list of refiners below.)

Refiners

Engelhard Industries, Div. of Engelhard Corporation
70 Wood Avenue South
Iselin, N.J. 08830

Handy & Harman
850 3rd Ave.
New York, N.Y. 10022

Johnson Mathey, Inc.
Malvern, Pa. 19355

N. L. Shteinshleifer Inc.
40 Elizabeth St.
New York, N.Y. 10013
(owned by Comptoir Lyon-Alemand Louyot, Paris, France, with other offices throughout Western Europe)

Generally speaking, you will realize a better potential profit margin on silver bullion if you purchase it in larger, rather than smaller, bars. Because of the bar charges mentioned in Chapter 2, it is less expensive for you to buy one 10-ounce bar than ten 1-ounce ones, and for that reason (unless you foresee an imminent currency collapse and want your silver in "small change"), I advise you to buy in the largest size you can afford. The cheapest per-ounce way to buy is to get a refinery's biggest bar, which today is the thousand-ounce bar; some refineries charge no premium at all on such a purchase. The next-best thing would be to buy 100-ounce bars, and so on.

Except for the very largest bars, you will always end up paying some premium above the spot-per-ounce price of the metal, and for this reason you should always shop around before buying. Most refiners charge about 3 to 4 percent above spot, meaning that on a 100-ounce bar when silver is $10 an ounce, you should expect to pay about $1,035 give or take a few dollars. You may be able to save money by comparing handling fees, so don't hesitate to do so. Most reputable dealers post their handling fees somewhere on their premises, so you don't even have to ask what they are, and those that don't follow this practice will still tell you what their fees are if you do ask. Be suspicious of anyone who won't let you know readily how much over spot you are being charged: dealers who "cannot give out this information" are usually the type who charge each person differently, depending on how much they think they can get away with.

Of course, one way of being sure that you don't get nickel-and-dimed to death with charges is to calculate, before you go in to buy, how much the silver should cost. Look up the day's spot price in the paper and multiply it by the number of ounces you want; you'll get an exact figure of how much the bullion itself should cost. If the price you are then quoted by a dealer is more than about 5 percent over this figure, take your business elsewhere.

Finally, you should inquire about your potential seller's buy-back policies. Johnson Mathey advertises an "unconditional buy-back guarantee at any time—based on current silver prices," and generally the major refiners offer the same guarantee. If you know that you can resell your bar to the same dealer at any time you please, you will be saved the aggravation of wondering how quickly you can get rid of an unwanted bar if the price slips, or how quickly you can do some profit taking if it rises. Even if you plan to hold on to your investment for a long time (this is the most prudent course), it is comforting to know that, if you need to raise money quickly at some time in the future, you can always sell some of your silver with no questions asked. Just be sure, when you ask about buy-back policies, that you find out how much of the day's spot price will be paid as well; because dealers have to make money, you won't ever get the full spot price, but you should avoid doing business with outfits that will not guarantee you any return at all.

OPTION 2: COINS AND MEDALLIONS

Because silver is so much more widespread than gold, and because it has always been used more extensively in coins, the world of silver coin collecting and trading is more complicated than that of gold coins. The same basic principles, as outlined in Chapter 2, apply to silver coins. Collectors grade silver coins just as they do gold coins; they distinguish between numismatic and bullion coins; and they pay varying premiums for numismatics, based on age, condition and rarity of the specimens. Beyond that, however, collecting silver coins diverges widely from collecting gold coins: there are so many silver coins around, and they come at such a relatively low price, that the field is awash with wrinkles that do not bother the more selective gold collectors.

One of the major wrinkles in silver coin collecting is that the line between numismatic and bullion coins is a little less distinct than it is in the case of gold. Depending on the spot price of silver, a coin could be considered a numismatic item one day and a coin fit only for melting the next. Nobody in his right mind, for example, would melt down a gold Double Eagle worth $1,000 just to get the $500 worth of gold it contains—such a coin, unless gold goes to over $1,000, will always be more valuable as a numismatic than as bullion. But in silver this is not always the case. Because the premium over bullion value is relatively low in silver coins, as the price of the metal fluctuates, a good numismatic can easily become worth more for its melt value than for its antique value—and it will thus be melted down. In fact, during the silver price hikes of the late 1970s, thousands of silver coins met just this fate: in a bullish silver market, they simply lost their value as collectibles.

This tendency for silver occasionally to outstrip its own premiums has an interesting, and beneficial, outcome for the investor. Not only can some collectors realize unexpected profits from selling their coins, but if you continue to hold on to silver coins, you will find that they will become ever more valuable—precisely because others have thought them worthless! With more coins going to the smelter, that leaves fewer coins in circulation—and that makes the remaining coins all the more valuable.

Many small investors have become aware of this paradoxical effect and have in the past several years flocked to purchase silver coins. According to Handy & Harman, at the end of the 1970s approximately half of the estimated 418 million ounces of silver being held by investors was in the form of silver coins.[2] The most common U.S. silver coins bought are the $1 (fine silver content: .76 troy oz.), the 1964 Kennedy half dollar (fine silver content: .36 troy oz.), the $.50 (fine silver content: .36 troy oz.), the $.25 (fine silver content: .175 troy oz.), and the $.10 (fine silver content: .07 troy oz.).

Of course, people are attracted to silver coins for the same reasons that they are attracted to gold coins: they are of historical interest and are often of artistic value. But the best thing about owning silver, rather than gold, in this form is that it is an option open to many more people. If you are investing for the beauty as well as the security, you will probably want to own several coins. In gold you would need a fair amount of money to do that: in silver, a mere $300 can buy you quite a few coins.

You can buy silver coins one by one, and if you are purchasing very old key-date numismatics, you will almost certainly buy them singly. But, for most silver coins, the common units of purchase are the roll and the bag. If you are buying old silver dollars, you may buy them in rolls of twenty. If you are buying something smaller, such as dimes, you will probably purchase a bag.

Let's look, for example, at a couple of the most popular old U.S. silver dollars, the Morgan dollar and the Peace dollar. Both of these coins were minted before 1965, so that they contain 90 percent silver and only 10 percent of alloy: this makes their silver content, per coin, a little over three quarters of an ounce. If you wanted to invest in this popular silver vehicle, how would you go about it?

If you bought from one of the major dealers, say New York City's Manfra Tordella & Brookes, you could buy them either singly or in rolls of twenty. You would specify that you wanted, say, a roll of 1883-O Morgan dollars in brilliant, uncirculated condition, or a roll of brilliant, uncirculated Peace dollars from 1923. You would check a price list[3] and compare offers before buying to see that you were being offered a fair deal. And when your silver was delivered—assuming you chose to take delivery—you would see that it was properly insured and safeguarded.

Alternatively, you could choose to buy a larger amount of less "desirable" coins. Perhaps you would want not BU coins, but merely fine or extra-fine specimens. Perhaps the key date would not be a major concern. You might just want to own silver coins, of almost any type, as an

[2] Quoted by Browne, op. cit.
[3] Lists appear in such publications as the *Investors Guide* and the various coin magazines. Be sure to consult the most recent figures.

investment bullion vehicle in the expectation of a silver price rise at some point in the future. If so, you could avoid paying the numismatic premium you would have to pay on a BU 1923 Peace dollar by buying coins of a smaller denomination but in a larger amount.

Say you have only a few hundred dollars to spend, and you see from your price list that that will buy you only one Morgan dollar. What you might do in this case is to purchase a bag of mixed coins: dimes, quarters and half dollars of no special key-date value but still containing 90 percent of silver and therefore still valuable as a bullion investment. Or you could buy a lot of pre-1965 dimes, mixed as to quality and date. In either case you would be buying coins of limited (but not negligible) numismatic value, but of fairly solid value as bullion.

The bags of coins being offered today vary in size and weight, and they are sold, generally, not by size or weight, but by the *face value* of the coins inside. This is an often confusing, but very important, point.

Say you decide to buy a "mini-bag" of dimes. This is the smallest bag now available. The face value of the silver coins inside will amount to $50, which means that your bag will contain 500 pre-1965 dimes. Or, at the other end of the scale, you might want to buy the largest available bag—with a face value of $1,000. In this case, you would get either 1,000 silver dollars, 2,000 half dollars, 4,000 quarters or possibly some mixture of these denominations.

In any case, note that you will be purchasing a set *number* of silver coins and paying for them according to that number. Even if you buy at the lowest available price, you will still pay more per ounce than the spot price of silver bullion. It would be wonderful if you could purchase a mini-bag of dimes for $50, but of course since the price of silver has risen substantially since the coins in such a bag were first minted, the price that you will pay will bear very little relation to the face value of the coins. Establishing face value is simply a convenient way for sellers to know how many coins you are getting: in fact at a $10 spot price for silver bullion, the worth of a $50 mini-bag would be something like $350 in actual bullion value.

But there is an advantage to this apparently high price for the coins. When you pay slightly over the bullion price for silver coins, you are betting that the silver price will rise in the future and that your coins therefore will go up even more in value—not even taking into consideration their possible numismatic increase. This may or may not happen. The silver price could fall. But—and here is the silver lining—no matter how much it falls, you cannot ever lose everything. Since the coins in your bag are not only a bullion investment, but negotiable currency as well, the lowest they can possibly ever fall in value is to the face value itself.

This means that, even if silver goes through the floor, the coins in your mini-bag will still be worth $50. The face value is a bottom price for your investment—and of course the likelihood that silver will fall that low is extremely slight. The much greater likelihood is that the floor will be merely a safety net and that your investment, *as bullion,* will continue to rise in value. If this happens, you would be in the happy position of the investor who needs to decide whether to hold on to his already valuable silver coins in the hopes that their collector value will rise, or sell them at a large bullion profit.

Now, although I have been speaking here of pre-1965 silver coins, the same basic principles also apply to items that do not fall into that category, such as commemorative coins and medallions, no matter when they were struck. Most people prefer to own pre-1965 silver coins, because it was in 1965 that the government stopped breaking even on the value of its coins and changed over to copper and nickel. Most coins minted since 1965, therefore, contain little or no silver and are not useful as investments. Most of these coins are "clad" coins composed of copper and nickel, and even most commemoratives that do contain silver—such as the Kennedy half dollar (silver content 40 percent, or .29 ounce) 1965 through 1969—are still lower in silver content than the pre-1965 halves.

What this means to you as an investor is that, whenever you are considering a purchase, you have to be sure exactly how much silver there is in your coin or medallion before you buy. Remember that the alloy is worthless as an investment and that, therefore, unless the item you have in mind has real numismatic value, you should keep away from items that are less than coin-grade (90 percent) silver. If you do buy something of a lower grade, you should pay a proportionately lower price.

This applies both to private-mint issues and to the less common government issues. No matter who mints your coin, be sure the price asked is not made up mostly of premium. Commemorative pieces tend to have very high premiums, and that's all right if you're a collector, but not if you're thinking of acquiring them as investments.

In a recent column, newspaperman Bob Greene called attention to the fact that, in the summer of 1982, the government issued its first commemorative half dollar in almost thirty years. Minted to honor the 250th anniversary of George Washington's birth, it's a .900 fine silver coin that sells, depending on whether you want the uncirculated or the proof version, for $8.50 or $10.50. Greene expressed astonishment at the fact that, in spite of this hefty charge, the coin will still buy only 50 cents' worth of goods at a store. The United States Mint advertised this coin on September 18, 1983, for $10, which is $5.66 over silver value—a markup of 130 percent. By comparison, the 1964 Kennedy half dollar was about 14 cents over silver value.

Greene needn't have been astonished. Items of this sort are sold not as legal tender (although they can be used as such), but as collectors' items. It's their supposed collector value that accounts for the $10.50 cost. The question you have to ask yourself is whether or not it's worth that extra cost: is the coin going to be rare enough in the future to justify paying a $5.66 premium for it now?

In the case of the Washington half, the answer is probably no. With ten million of them being minted, it's unlikely they will ever become so rare that their numismatic value will soar—though of course their bullion value might increase. But here again, that increase will probably not justify the price. A 50-cent piece of this type contains only .3617 ounce of silver—and at today's silver price, that is worth $4.34.

Why do people buy these things, then? There are a lot of answers to that, including collecting mania, the desire to own silver at any cost and simple patriotism. Many people buy such items as a kind of civic gesture, because they know it will help the government out. I won't say you shouldn't buy such a commemorative for any of these reasons; but just remember that, as investment or numismatic items, these coins are not the best bets.

The same thing goes double for many of the private-mint medallions. Private mints almost always charge such a high premium for their creations that the price becomes prohibitive unless you are an avid collector. The same caution that I advised in purchasing gold medallions applies for silver ones too. The rule of thumb is to know, before you shop, how much pure bullion is selling for, so you can calculate what percentage of the offered price is merely a dealer's markup.

The Sunshine Mining Company, for example, recently minted a one-ounce silver piece that it hopes small investors will buy instead of bullion. It's an attractive coin, and you might want to consider it as an alternative to owning bars or wafers. But before you buy, check your figures. One ounce of solid silver in this form will inevitably cost you more than the same ounce in a wafer. If it's only a matter of a few cents more, you may want the more attractive coin. But if a dealer offering you the Sunshine coin wants 20 or 30 percent above spot, it won't be a wise investment.

On certain silver offerings, the premium can be even higher than that; these offerings you should steer clear of, even when they look attractive.

The private Buckingham Mint, for example, offered four "silver ace ingots" of .999 silver at a total cost of $21. Their ad, which I saw in *TV Guide,* stated the actual weight and fineness, but unless you knew what to look for, you could easily have come away with the impression that you were buying in on a real bargain. Which was definitely not the case.

The four "ingots" weighed a "hefty" two grams each, which made the combined weight of the silver eight grams. One troy ounce contains a little over 31 grams. This means that the eight grams of silver being offered here weighed just about a quarter of an ounce. With silver at $6.00 an ounce (the approximate price at the time of the ad), this means that the four ingots contained a total of $1.50 worth of silver. And they were being sold for $21! For them to be worth that much money as bullion, silver would have to go to $84 an ounce—a figure it didn't reach even in the wildest days of 1979.

But of course the ingots weren't being sold as bullion. They were being sold as jewelry. Indeed, for an extra four dollars you could buy a silver chain to hang them on, and because they were being sold as jewelry, buyers had to pay a premium of almost twenty dollars. As we'll see in Chapter 11 of this book, that's not uncommon in the jewelry business.

The lesson of all this is simple. When you are shopping around for silver, you have to keep in mind that the farther away you get from pure, uncomplicated bullion—that is, the more workmanship that has to go into the item—the more premium you are going to pay. That is why, as a pure bullion investment, nothing can beat silver bars. This is not to say that you shouldn't buy those ingots if you like them. If you find such an offer attractive as jewelry, by all means purchase a set. Just don't fool yourself into thinking that you're making a bullion investment.

OPTION 3: SILVERWARE

Exactly the same principle applies when you are shopping for silver flatware or silver hollowware. Here again a good deal of the value lies not in the bullion content of the tea service or punchbowl, but in its antique or collectible value. And that value depends on factors that are totally unknown to the novice silver collector. While it is often true that the older a piece is, the more valuable it is, you should not enter the complicated world of silverware trading with only that minimum information.

In buying and selling silverware, just as in buying and selling old coins, it is clearly to your advantage to do your homework before you jump in. If you're interested in buying Georgian silver, you should go to the library first and read up on Georgian hallmarks, familiarize yourself with common reproductions, compare price lists for specific items and in general shop around. The more you know before you buy, the less likely you are to end up a victim of your own ignorance. There are numerous good price guides available in this tricky field, and you should definitely at least browse through a couple of them before committing yourself to a purchase.

I have said that premium is important in this field, and that is so, but only up to a point. One of the ironies of the silverware field is that many of the pieces considered antiques, because of silver's rise in price since they were made, can become more valuable as bullion than as historical items. For this reason, even though you may have bought that teaspoon set as an antique, you may find, a couple of years from now, that it is more valuable to you as bullion. You may find that you can get more for it from a scrap dealer—who will have it melted down—than you can from an antique dealer.

This is a sad but important fact. As silver rises in value, even quite old pieces of silverware are constantly being melted down. When the price reached $50 during the 1979–80 madness, I saw two-hundred-year-old pieces being melted down—and pieces of lesser venerability (much Victoriana, for example) reach the smelter's pot long before that.

This has a double effect, just as the melting of old coins has a double effect. First, it temporarily reduces the antique value of the old silver: when you see your neighbor get $200 from a refiner for a teapot that the antique market appraises at $150, you are going to be much more eager to unload your own antiques. Second, it eventually *increases* the antique value of the remaining pieces: as more George III teaspoons get melted down, the ones that remain become all the rarer, and hence more valuable.

It is this seesaw effect between bullion value and collectible value that governs a great deal of what goes on in the silver flatware and silver hollowware market. This is especially true today, when the worldwide demand for silver continues to outstrip production, and buyers look ever more frequently to unconventional sources of the metal—such as antique shops and attic storerooms.

When you buy silverware today, remember that your purchase might end up melted down—and that therefore the "antique" premium you pay on it may turn out to have been irrelevant. This is less true, naturally, of very old or very distinguished items—a fourteenth-century chalice, for example, or a Paul Revere tankard. Nobody is going to melt them down unless silver is hugely overinflated, and as a result buying such pieces even at a high antique premium is almost always justified, providing you can afford it. More recent pieces, like that 1890s saltcellar you were holding on to in hopes of an auction, may end up being more valuable to you as bullion. This is especially so right now, when the collectibles market is relatively depressed, while the demand for industrial silver remains strong.

Therefore, you should calculate how much premium you can afford to pay on an antique silver item, assuming that antiques will grow slowly in value and silver bullion somewhat faster. If you can buy that table setting for even 20 or 30 percent over the spot price of its silver content, then I'd say you were still investing wisely. Silver will almost certainly continue to rise at 10 percent or so a year, so that if you hold on to the setting for a few years, you will very likely keep pace with inflation. Just remember to calculate in dealers' costs and inflation when you determine whether or not the purchase will be a sound one. And of course, if you are buying the setting as a potential bullion investment, you must calculate its potential value in terms not of its total weight, but of its silver content alone.

Discovering what that content is, as we'll see in the next chapter, can sometimes be a difficult task, and that is why I urge you again, as soon as you have decided to invest in silverware, to deal only with a known, reliable person. In the next chapter you'll see why that advice is so crucial.

OPTION 4: SILVER FUTURES

Dealing in silver futures is not really very different from dealing in gold futures, since the same basic terms apply to both fields. Hedging, buying on margin, offsetting—all these factors operate in silver just as they do in gold, and if you are interested in silver futures I advise you first to read the last section of Chapter 2 if you have not already done so. It will explain to you the basic principles, and risks, involved not only in precious-metals trading, but in any futures speculation.

Some small investors are attracted to silver futures speculation under the false assumption that, because silver is so much lower than gold in value, they can get into this market a lot more cheaply, and with less risk, than they could get into gold. This is not the case. The standard gold futures contract, you may recall, is for 100 troy ounces of the metal. This would sell for $40,000 (when gold is at $400 an ounce), of which a portion would have to be paid in front, as a margin. The standard silver futures contract, on the other hand, is for 5,000 ounces. With silver at $10 an ounce, you would pay $50,000, which is more than the cost of 100 ounces of gold. And you'd have to come up with the same margin. So silver futures are not really a "poor man's" market.

Nor is this the only problem with silver futures. It's true that silver is less volatile than gold, more likely to retain its steady price rise in the future. But that does not mean that you cannot lose by speculating in silver. There are no sure things in the futures markets. If there were, the Hunt brothers would not have lost an estimated one billion dollars there. My advice to you is to be cautious, and to begin your initial forays into silver in a less volatile and less expensive market—such as buying bullion, coins or silverware.

There are problems in these fields too, of course, and we'll look at some of them now.

CHAPTER 6

THE SMART SILVER SHOPPER

In Chapter 3, I noted various practices that unscrupulous dealers use to defraud the unwary purchaser of gold. Virtually all of these practices—including assaying tricks, forgery, price juggling and the imposition of a high dealer's fee—are used to cheat the innocent silver buyer as well, and for that reason I suggest, before you read this chapter, that you go back and skim Chapter 3 again, to familiarize yourself with the basic caveats that a buyer of any precious metal must observe.

Remember that I said the first thing you have to decide, when you are about to buy precious metals, is who your source will be—and that, in doing this, caution should be your watchword. All the firms that now sell gold—banks, brokerage houses, metals dealers, jewelers and mail-order firms—also sell silver, and if you're buying the white metal, the same principles of selection apply. The rule of thumb is to deal only with known, well-established people, and preferably people whose reputation can be checked out with the Better Business Bureau, the Securities and Exchange Commission or both. The more you know about the person you're dealing with, the less likely it is you'll be cheated. So don't be afraid to investigate before you buy: it's your money, and you have a right to know that your party is reliable before you hand it over.

Remember, too, that you should always *shop around* before you commit your money to any investment, be it silver, gold or anything else. Even the most reputable dealers have varying fees and handling charges, and it's to your advantage to do business with the one who will give you the best arrangement for your money—that is, the one from whom you can buy your silver as closely as possible to the spot price of the metal. Even if you're buying only a few silver coins, there's no point in paying a dealer a 50 percent commission on them if you can buy exactly the same thing down the street for one tenth of that premium.

If you're primarily interested in silver, rather than gold, you will be happy to learn that there is a marginally smaller chance that you will run into unscrupulous dealers in the first place. Or, to put it more precisely, the people who commonly cheat the public in precious metals tend to do so more frequently in gold than in silver, because there is

more profit in gold. Selling a gold-plated coin as if it were pure gold
might net the dealer a three- or four-hundred-dollar profit, while passing off a silver-plated coin as solid will net him one tenth that much.
Buying the less expensive metal, therefore, has its built-in advantages,
since the big-time cheats tend to favor the big kills, rather than strings
of smaller deceptions.

But this definitely does not mean that buying silver is without its
dangers. Not all cheats are big-timers, and you can easily be taken to
the cleaners even if you're only out to spend a couple of hundred dollars. When you're buying the "poor man's gold," there are always
plenty of people who are out to ensure that you stay poor while you're
doing so. Here are some of the tricks they use.

COUNTERFEITING: COINS

If you do business only with established, reputable firms, there is little
chance you will end up buying a forged coin or a bar of silver that is less
pure than it is marked. If you buy from a smaller dealer, however, you
are treading on shakier ground. In spite of the smaller profit margin, the
counterfeiting of silver coins is by no means uncommon. As I mentioned earlier, the American Numismatic Association Certification Service noted recently that about one third of the coins they were asked to
analyze generally turn out to be faked. Naturally, not all of these coins
are gold: many are ancient silver "bargains" that, when analyzed, turn
out to be of dubious vintage, short in weight or both. Numismatic
collecting has gained enormously in popularity in recent years, and
since most collectors concentrate on silver, rather than gold, coins, it
would be strange indeed if unethical minters and dealers didn't take
advantage of their interest.

That is why, if you're just starting out collecting silver coins, it's wise
to begin by reading as much as possible about the field before you
purchase anything. If you're buying straight bullion from Engelhard or
a recent medallion from the Franklin Mint, you don't have too much to
worry about in terms of the quality of the product. But if you're buying
coins, there's always that numismatic premium factor to take into account. Because numismatics always command a significant premium
over the bullion content, you can easily be taken in if you haven't done
your homework.

You might, for example, be interested in buying a roll of pre-1965
dimes, and you might be unlucky enough to run across a dealer who
tries to convince you that "a dime is a dime is a dime." If you haven't

read up on dimes before you shop, you could end up buying a roll of Roosevelt dimes at Mercury prices. Since Mercury dimes now command about three times as much from collectors as Roosevelt dimes, the loss could be substantial.

This kind of scam can work in reverse, too. I remember the sad story of a young man a couple of years ago who, eager to raise some ready cash, brought in three uncirculated Liberty quarters to an unethical dealer. The dealer offered him $450 for the three of them, and brought out an "official" price list to prove that this was a fair offer: sure enough, the list indicated that a Liberty quarter in uncirculated condition was at that time worth $150. The young man took the cash happily, overjoyed that the dealer, out of the kindness of his heart, wasn't even charging him a commission.

What the young man didn't know—he discovered it later, to his chagrin—was that there are two types of Liberty quarters, one showing the figure of Liberty standing, and the other showing her head alone: this latter coin, known as the "Barber" Liberty, after the person who designed it, is worth almost two times as much to collectors as the standing Liberty version, and it was the Barber coin that the dealer had paid such a "good" price for. Since the young man was ignorant of the difference between the two coins, the dealer had been able to pay him a standing Liberty price for the three Barber coins. Even counting a dealer's commission, what the young man *should* have received for them was about $800. So in effect he lost $350.

Know what you're getting into, therefore, before you shop for silver coins. Your local library should have several volumes devoted to the prices of these popular investments, and you should definitely check one out before you buy. Or you can purchase the latest edition of the *Blackbook Price Guide of U.S. Coins,* from the House of Collectibles, at 1900 Premier Row, Orlando, Florida, 32809. It costs $2.50, which is a very moderate outlay for something that might save you a good deal of grief, not to mention money.

Not all frauds are as direct as this one. Some involve actual debasement or disfigurement of the coins; these are much more difficult to discern. Since the value of numismatics depends so much on the specifics of mintage and place of origin, you will sometimes come across coins that have been subtly tampered with in order to increase their value. Probably the most common example of this kind of fraud is the alteration of a mint mark. The small "D" that indicates Denver might be added to a coin without a mint mark because the Denver issues are more valuable. Or a mint mark might be removed. Coins without a mint mark were minted in Philadelphia, and since some Philadelphia coins are quite rare, removing a mark could increase the supposed value of a coin.

Again, dealing with a reliable, known dealer is your best insurance against practices of this sort. Knowing your terrain before you buy is an absolute essential. If you're not dealing with a known person, carry your magnifying glass with you and check the mint marks carefully against pictures of the coins in your price guide. Very tiny discrepancies between the coin you want and the ·picture may indicate nothing, or they may indicate that you have a forged item. In cases in which you are uncertain, it's always good to be wary—and if possible to get a second opinion. When you get around to reselling your "great find," you may be sure that the new buyer will be rigorous in weeding out even potential forgeries. You should be no less rigorous.

All of this applies as well to buying and selling silverware, and it's silverware counterfeiting that we want to look at now.

COUNTERFEITING: SILVERWARE

Great Britain is one of the most famous sources of fine old silver, and the government has always taken silversmithing very seriously there. Because silverwork was highly prized—and of course because the relationship was always close between silverware and silver coinage—the British Government has always taken a dim view of silver fraud. In 1238, Henry III issued an ordinance concerning the quality of gold and silver wares to be used by goldsmiths, and in 1327 the Guild of London Goldsmiths became officially incorporated under a royal charter granted by Edward III. According to Seymour Wyler's *The Book of Old Silver,* in some instances the penalty for tampering with regulated, hallmarked silver was death, and for this reason, there has traditionally not been very much antiquated forged silver available in England. As Wyler observes, "As quickly as the government punished the offender, so it destroyed his wares."

But one could not expect forgery to be totally absent from a field that is potentially as lucrative as the silver trade, and in spite of the death penalty, some forgeries did slip by. In these more enlightened times, moreover, where a forger need not fear the loss of his head, the practice of debasing and altering silverware has not subsided. If your primary interest is in silver objects other than coins, therefore, it's important for you to know what kind of dishonest practices you may encounter in this area.

Wyler notes two basic types of fraud that have always been the most common in silver trading. The first is the physical transformation of the object in question, and the second is the transformation of the hallmark.

In transforming a silver object, forgers employ several common techniques; although these techniques are somewhat less common today, you may still run into them in the antiques market, and they can seriously affect an object's value. The major techniques are subtraction, addition and full-scale transformation.

In *subtraction,* part of the original object is removed: If a customer wants a silver cup, for example, but the dishonest dealer has only an urn, he will remove the spout from the urn and sell the remaining, debased object as a cup. (It *is* a cup, of course, but it is no longer an original antique, and the dealer has no right to charge an antique price for it.) In *addition,* the reverse occurs: the forger adds a spout, for example, to satisfy the demand of a customer who wants an urn. In *transformation,* the entire object is altered: A tray may be hammered and reshaped into a platter or a bowl. This was the case, I discovered to my chagrin, with a punch bowl I bought in London in the 1940s. It was stamped with an 1805 hallmark, but it turned out to be only half as valuable as I thought it was at the time, because it had been transformed from a tray.

There is really nothing wrong with refashioning objects in this way, provided the customer knows what he or she is getting. In many cases, this is not so. A woman I knew a few years ago purchased what she thought was a vintage Queen Anne butter dish; she was attracted to it particularly because of the peculiar curvature of the "feet" that constituted its base. She paid a price for it that would have been pretty reasonable if in fact the piece had been as old as she thought. The trouble was that the particular curvature that attracted her was not introduced into silverwork until fifty years after Queen Anne died—which meant that the woman had paid a champagne price for an object that was at least partly still wine. The "feet" that had attracted her had been added on later, and so the piece—as pretty as it was—could not be considered genuine.

She could have avoided being taken in this fashion if she had done her homework beforehand. This applies just as much to silverware as it does to coins. Before you shop, consult. If you're in the market for Sheffield silver, go to the library first. Get out a book on Sheffield and familiarize yourself with what items were made there, by whom and when. Check out a current price list, and form a general idea of a "ballpark" figure for the item in which you're interested. Only after you have done all this should you actually put down money.

Your homework should include some study of silverworkers' hallmarks. A hallmark is an officially approved "signature" put on a finished piece of silver at an assay office after it has been assayed and after the required duties have been paid. Each silversmith had his own, registered mark, and it is these marks that often give a piece its ultimate store of value. Because there are so many of them, you really need to consult a guide before jumping to the conclusion that a marked piece is automatically valuable.

The bible for identifying English hallmarks is Sir Charles J. Jackson's *English Goldsmiths and Their Marks,* which is published by Dover. I urge you to consult it before buying any supposed "antique." The mere fact that a piece is hallmarked does not necessarily mean it is valuable. You have to determine also what the hallmark indicates (about date, silver content and maker) and then whether or not it is authentic. The forging of hallmarks is not uncommon—which is another good argument for dealing only with reputable shops and dealers.

Here too, the more you know, the better off you will be. Most Americans, for example, know that Paul Revere was noted in his day not as a night-riding militiaman, but as a silversmith. "Revere Ware" remains to this day one of the nation's proudest craft achievements, and if you are lucky enough to own something done by the hand of Paul Revere, you can be pretty certain that its price will continue to rise: Revere Ware is not among the types of silver that are swiftly melted down during a bullion price rise.

But few people realize that the hallmark "Revere," even if it is absolutely authentic, does not necessarily refer to the work of the noted hero of Longfellow's poem. Many of Revere's relatives were also silversmiths, and in fact both his father and his son were named not only Revere, but Paul as well. This means that a piece that is marked "PR" may or may not have been created by the Revolutionary War hero. It may have been created by his father or his son—which would mean that it would still be valuable, but not nearly as valuable as one made by the famous Revere himself.

This is the kind of information you can find out from a hallmark guide such as Wyler's, and obviously the more of it you know, the better you will be able to bargain with the dealer who tells you the teaspoons you have your eye on are "without question" the work of Master So-and-so and are therefore worth your next month's wages.

Of course, hallmarks themselves are forged, because that's the quickest way to increase the price of an item without changing the item itself. For reasons that we've noted, this is not so common on older pieces, but it's not at all rare on newer pieces. Old hallmarks are sometimes placed on newer pieces after being "lifted" from a spoon. The hallmark is cut out of the spoon and welded into a bowl or tray so carefully that only an expert can detect the fraud.

In other instances, the "sterling" stamp itself is forged. For example, a teapot that is actually made of only 80 percent silver will be stamped "sterling," indicating that it contains 92.5 percent. The only way you can uncover devious stamping like this is to have the metal tested, and if you are at all uncertain about the silver content of a piece that interests you, by all means arrange to have that done.

But this gets us into the area of assaying and testing melt value—another area in which dishonesty sometimes prevails. Let's look now at how the unethical in the silver world defraud not with the externals of their wares, but with the metal itself.

ASSAYING TRICKS

I mentioned in Chapter 3 that dishonest dealers will frequently "short-weight" items so that they can get away with paying you less for your gold than it is actually worth. They do this by using dishonest scales and by knowingly misstating the purity of the metal. The same thing happens with silver.

One way you can get around these practices is to have your item assayed independently before you sell, if the potential selling price justifies an assay fee. If it does not, at least weigh the item yourself, and figure on the basis of the day's spot price about how much you should get for it. If you're selling silver coins, know about how much they're worth before you enter the shop, so that if the dealer tells you a 1958 coin has only 30 percent of silver in it, you can nod politely as you back out the door. If you're selling a hallmarked silver tray, look up the hallmark first, so that you won't be taken in by somebody claiming that a Queen Anne piece was "really" made in 1892.

If you have any question about the honesty of a shop's weighing procedures, ask to see the state's official seal of inspection on the scale. Many states require such inspection, and a dealer who does not prominently display a seal—or who is reluctant to point it out to you—may have something to hide. An honest dealer should be proud to point out this official certification of his honesty; if your dealer isn't, take your trade somewhere else.

Assaying tricks such as short-weighting are particularly common in the silver trade, because so much silver is (or is thought to be) not solid silver or even coin silver, but silver-plated wares. There are special problems associated with plated silverware; you should know about them before you either buy or sell.

The main problem with plate is that the silver (that is, the bullion) content of a plated item is almost never of any consequence. Around 1825, the electroplating process began to replace the old art of welding a sheet of silver to a sheet of copper (such welded pieces were known as "old Sheffield"), and although sterling pieces continued to be made throughout the nineteenth century, they were vastly outnumbered by the new electroplated pieces. Some of these electroplated silver objects have some antiquarian value, but none of them have any bullion value. So you have to be very careful when a dealer tries to sell you plated silverware as an "investment" in the metal itself. Almost certainly, the bulk of the item's weight will be that of its inner core of plaster, lead or other heavy material.

This is a problem when you try to sell your silverware too. The necessity of estimating the silver-bullion weight of silverware leads to fraud in the case of many purchases of "loaded hollow ware"—that is, pieces that are sterling silver but that are weighted inside. When you go to sell such an item, whether it's a candlestick or a saltshaker, you are always in danger of being shortchanged.

Rather than estimating the weight of the silver, an honest dealer will knock out the weighting plaster and weigh the remaining scrap. A dishonest dealer will say he has to estimate and give you an estimate he knows is low. Naturally this will dramatically drive down the price you'll be offered for the piece.

One last trick you should be familiar with—one that you might encounter not when you sell an item but when you buy one. I mentioned in Chapter 5 that the three most common grades of silver are sterling (.925), coin silver (.900), and Britannia (.958). If you shop for silverware very often, there is one other type of "silver" you may run across, and that is German silver. Actually, this is a misnomer, because there is virtually no silver content in it. But selling "German silver" as silver has proved to be one of the most durable of silver frauds.

By "German silver" I don't mean simply silver made in Germany: this is usually .800 fine, and so marked. What is often sold as "German silver" is actually composed of nickel, zinc and copper. The amount of silver in it is infinitesimal, usually accounting for less than 1 percent of the total weight. This curious, nonsilver "silver" was used extensively in German-made trinkets in the mid-nineteenth century and was frequently sold to the unwary, who thought they were purchasing good silver. When an 1890 U.S. law stipulated that imports had to be stamped, many items made of this alloy were dutifully stamped "German silver," and the term has continued to this day.

If you are offered an item that is stamped "German silver," do not believe the seller who tells you that it is an exotic and very rare species of the metal. As Marc Hudgeons notes, "The common reference to it as 'low grade' silver is misleading; it should more correctly be called 'no grade.' "[1]

THE PRICE GAME

To buy and sell silver successfully at the retail level, you have to be able to convince the dealer that what you have is so valuable that he should pay almost any price for it—while what he has for you is so trivial that he should thank you for taking it off his hands. Obviously there's a great deal of game playing in this field, and the "game" is generally won not necessarily by the person who has the more valuable item, but by the one who best knows its "real" price compared with the prices of other items in the field.

You can increase your chances of coming out ahead in the "price game" if you keep a few simple guidelines in mind. Many of these, I've already mentioned in reference to gold, but they bear repeating here:

▪ Be aware first that the price of silver, like that of gold, is "fixed" each day and that the fixed daily price—the daily spot—is published in the newspapers. Always check this price before you buy or sell, and do not agree to deal with someone who offers you a per-ounce price for your silver that is less favorable than the official quote. Both Engelhard and Handy & Harman set daily spots in this country, and they differ slightly from each other. Be sure that you do not, on the same day, agree to buy at the higher rate and sell at the lower. (The reverse, of course, is the ideal.)

▪ Weigh your silver before you buy or sell, and calculate before you enter any transactions how much you should expect to get or give. Having this figure in mind before you go into a shop will cut down on unnecessary dickering and enable you to excuse yourself quickly from those establishments where the spot quoted, the weight given or both are off base. Do not be taken in by dealers who claim your silver is "too old" or "too tarnished" to justify the spot. If it's silver, and not plate, it's worth the spot—minus a reasonable commission and the value of the alloy content.

[1] Hudgeons, op. cit.

▪ Unless you're dealing with a very old firm, ask for payment in cash, rather than check. Fly-by-night operations have multiplied enormously in recent years, and you will avoid being left with a rubber check from one of these places if you insist on cash.

▪ Expect to pay a healthy dealer's fee on any silver transaction you make. If you are selling old silver for scrap, you might reasonably pay as much as 20 percent as commission: that is, if you sell $100 worth of silver teaspoons and they are to be melted, expect to get about $80 or a little more for them. Many dealers, of course, take much higher commissions than this, which is why you should shop around before committing yourself. A dealer deserves his commission, but he does not deserve to get rich off your ignorance.

▪ If you are selling something that could reasonably be thought to have antique or collectible value, check whether it would be better to sell it as scrap or as an antique. This goes for coins as well as teaspoons. Don't get caught in the sorry situation of selling an item for melt value and finding out in next week's paper that the dealer you sold it to just put it up for auction at a reserve price five times what you got for it. The basic rule here is to know what you're buying or selling—and to know how much of the item is bullion value and how much is over and above that.

Finally, a comment that comprises all the above and more: the principal thing to remember, as you set out to play the silver price game, is to let the dealer believe that *you know as much as, or more than, he does.*

This will seldom be the case, of course, but the dealer doesn't have to know that. The point you have to remember is that, no matter how much the *intrinsic* value of a coin or a silver tea set, what really matters is the ultimate *traded* price—and that price is determined just as much by what you and the dealer *think* about an item's worth as by what the weights and price lists say. Naturally the dealer will attempt to buy as low and sell as high as he can—that's why he's in business. What you have to do is to beat him at his own game, by holding out for the best selling price you can and buying at the lowest he will offer.

I don't mean this to sound insidious or ruthless. Buying and selling precious metals can be a great deal of fun—but it is a game, remember, in which the stakes are relatively high. For that reason, it should be taken seriously, and the way to take it seriously is to learn all the rules before you begin, and then deal honestly, but firmly, with the dealer.

Your honesty does not have to extend to telling him exactly what you know and don't know. On the contrary, one of the basic techniques of this price game is that you should display the knowledge you have and conceal the fact that it's limited. Do not enter a jeweler's shop with your grandmother's silver brooch and say, "I don't know what this is worth. How much would you say?" That's an invitation to an unscrupulous dealer to cut the actual value in half and "do you the favor" of buying. Do not walk into a shop with your bankroll out and say, "Gee, that's a lovely medallion. I bet it's worth a lot, huh?" Again, that's an invitation to be cheated. Beware also of buyers who ask *you* to name a price, hoping that you'll start low; a reputable dealer who takes a fair profit on each sale (rather than "adjusting" that profit for each customer) will be happy to quote you a figure on the ring or coin you want to sell. He won't ask you to "guess" at its worth, thus displaying your own ignorance.

Most dealers in silver are honest, and if you find one of them, this chapter can be safely tucked away in the back of your mind. If you deal in silver long enough, though, you are bound to come across a bad egg, and it's to guard against becoming his victim that I've laid out the dangers above. Whomever you deal with, though, one basic principle stands, for silver no less than for gold: the more you know *beforehand,* the better trader you will be.

PART **III**

THE PRINCE OF GEMS

CHAPTER 7
FROM FIRE TO ICE

One day late in the year 1866, a fifteen-year-old South African boy named Erasmus Jacobs was walking along a riverbank near his family's farm when he noticed a stone near the water. It sparkled strangely in the sunlight, and thinking to make a present of it to his sister, Erasmus picked it up and put it in his pocket. His sister was delighted with the gift but tired of it shortly, and the children's mother casually gave it away to a trader named Schalk van Niekerk. Suspecting that the stone was a diamond, he had it appraised in nearby Grahamstown and eventually sold it to the governor of Cape Colony, who shipped it to London to be displayed at the Paris Universal Exposition.

The stone that Erasmus had picked up had by this time been given a name—the Eureka Diamond—and was shortly cut into a finished gem weighing a little under eleven carats. Of the money realized from its sale, Schalk van Niekerk received 350 pounds, which was quite a sum in those days for a stone. He offered half of this sum to Erasmus' father, but the Boer farmer turned him down, saying that he could not accept money for a pebble.

Nobody understood at the time that the Jacobs boy's find was to be only the first in a fabulous string of diamond discoveries that, within a very few years, would make the banks of the Orange River a madhouse of mining activity. The Eureka Diamond was only the tip of a huge iceberg of precious crystals that, when extracted from the earth, would soon make South Africa the center of world diamond mining. Within ten years after the Jacobs family refused their share of the Eureka profits, the very word "diamond" had become indelibly associated with the names Kimberley and Bloemfontein and De Beers. Henceforth, when people thought of the beautiful gems, they would think automatically of South Africa.

It had not always been so. Diamonds had been mined before, in places far afield from South Africa. In the eighteenth century, the world home of diamond mining had been Brazil, and so important was the industry to the region that, a generation before the Eureka find, the Brazilian colony of Tejuco had been renamed Diamantina. In the five years between 1730 and 1735, slaves extracted so many diamonds from Brazilian rivers that the average world price for the uncut gems dropped by three quarters because of overproduction.

And before Brazil there had been India. Not much is heard about India in the diamond market today, but in the ancient world the subcontinent held a virtual monopoly on the production of the gems. It was from the great diamond mines at Golconda, in central India, that Arab traders brought the sparkling gems to Europe from antiquity through the Middle Ages. It was certainly an Indian diamond that the Roman historian Pliny had in mind when he noted (quite wrongly) that, when placed on an anvil and hit with a hammer, the gem would shatter both hammer and anvil before breaking itself. And of course many of the world's most famous diamonds—including the Koh-i-noor, the Orlov, and the Hope—came originally from Indian mines.

The diamond's peculiar hardness, too—as Pliny's exaggeration makes clear—had also been known since ancient times; it was this hardness that created the peculiar reflective capacity that made the gem so valued by ancient peoples. In northern Indian Buddhism, the diamond has long been a symbol of imperishability, and the very word for the gem in Greek—*adamas*—means, literally, "hardness."

So the Eureka discovery did not bring anything really new into the world, in terms of knowledge of the mineral. What it brought, however, in terms of the marketing and general availability of the gems, was immensely significant. Before the 1870s, diamonds were a true luxury item, owned only by the very wealthy and used almost exclusively in jewelry. Once the South African industry got under way, however, many nonjewelry uses for the stones were found, and even in the field of jewelry, diamonds became a commodity that was seen in some of the most modest homes. Because of what happened along the Orange River, the gems ceased to be the exclusive property of royalty and the upper classes.

There were two main reasons for this: The first has to do with the way the gems were mined—and are still mined—in South Africa.

In Brazil, and in many of the Indian mines too, the chief method of "extraction" was simply to wash the rough stones out of alluvial (river) deposits. Most diamonds in these two areas were, like the Eureka diamond, alluvial finds: that is, they were found lying on or very near the surface of the ground, generally along riverbanks, where the water had deposited them along with a lot of far less valuable silt. You got at such diamonds the same way you got at alluvial gold: with pans and sieves and other "sifting" tools.

In South Africa, however, alluvial gathering of diamonds lasted only a few years. Before long, many of the surface diamonds were all found, and the infant South African industry might have folded up its tents and gone home—except that, at this point, a far richer method of accumulation was discovered. As you probably know, diamonds are formed deep beneath the earth's surface when carbon is subjected to enormous heat and pressure so that it crystallizes into what is the world's hardest substance: a diamond is simply carbon in this crystallized form. The diamond, thus formed, is then carried toward the surface of the earth in conduits of a volcanic rock known as kimberlite. These conduits are called *pipes,* and the great discovery of the South African mining industry in the late-nineteenth century was that these pipes, containing both kimberlite and diamonds, could be mined directly as well.

That is, you no longer had to wait until the diamond-bearing kimberlite reached the earth's surface and water and wind erosion exposed the precious gems to view. You could dig into the earth directly and take the gems out of the pipes. That is the type of mining that South Africa began to specialize in, and it quickly yielded not only a much more copious source of diamonds, but diamonds of a much higher quality as well.

To get an idea of the richness of this new mining method, you have only to think of the "Big Hole" near Kimberley. This was the first major pipe to be exploited, and it proved so thick with gems that it was still being worked up until the First World War. Today, at fifteen hundred feet wide and over thirty-six hundred feet deep, the exhausted hole is the largest excavated crater in the world.

Mining "directly" by digging is, of course, a much more expensive method than picking up stones from the ground, and this is so not only because of labor costs, but because for each carat of diamond that a mine yields, you must extract many tons of nonprecious ore: the kimberlite pipes are rich, but they are far from being pure diamond. On the average, you may have to dig out three or four tons of ore for every rough carat you produce. That is one reason that diamonds are so expensive. But no one doubts that this procedure is worth the effort, for pipe mining is still the most lucrative method of extracting the precious crystals, and South Africa is still the source of the finest gems. It no longer produces a majority of the world's diamonds, but it does produce a majority of the investment-quality and gem-quality stones.

Development of pipe mining was only the first reason that South Africa became preeminent in diamond production. The other reason had to do with the marketing of the stones that were produced; to understand how diamonds are marketed, you must know something about what people in the business call the Syndicate.

THE SYNDICATE

No other commodity in the world is more firmly established in the public mind with a single name than diamonds are established with the name "De Beers." It is impossible to talk about the marketing of diamonds without talking about De Beers, and for that reason, many people suppose that the De Beers family was principally responsible for developing the modern diamond market. This is not the case. Actually the De Beers family had almost nothing to do with marketing diamonds, and it is ironic that the best-known name in the field is that of a pair of brothers who were well out of the diamond business before marketing began in earnest.

D. A. and J. N. De Beers merely owned the farm on which, in 1871, a major diamond find occurred. In the frenzy of those early years, the brothers were forced to vacate their property rather quickly, before they were literally overrun by gem-hungry prospectors, and although they received a fairly substantial sum for the farm (sixty three hundred pounds), they retained no interest in the land, and it was only because it had long been called the De Beers place that the mine which soon opened on it came to be called the De Beers mine as well.

One of the early part owners of the De Beers mine was an ambitious, visionary Englishman named Cecil Rhodes, and it was the tireless Rhodes who consolidated many of the small mines in the area, bought up as many claims as he could, and in 1881 founded the De Beers Mining Company. Rhodes was enormously successful in moving toward his dream of monopolizing the South African diamond industry, and by 1888 only one man, a colorful Cockney named Barney Barnato, stood in the way of Rhodes's complete control. Barnato owned the powerful Kimberley Central Mining Company, then the largest mine in the area, and Rhodes realized that, unless he could reach an agreement with him, the two might end up cutting into each other's profits by creating undesirable competition. The agreement was reached on March 13, 1888, when Barnato's and Rhodes's companies merged into a new organization, De Beers Consolidated Mines, Ltd. Today's De Beers organization is the outgrowth of that infant giant.

As his choice of terms might indicate, it was Rhodes's ambition to consolidate all diamond operations in South Africa under one umbrella —and to hold on to that umbrella himself. In that endeavor he was largely successful, but his success was nothing compared to the success that his company has had since his death in controlling not only diamond production, but diamond marketing and distribution as well. Not only does De Beers Consolidated today remain the single largest producer of rough diamonds; it also controls much of the non-South African production by buying up as much as it can of diamonds from South America, the Soviet Union and other parts of Africa. In addition, it is the principal force setting the *price* of rough diamonds on the world market—not only because of its control of supply, but also because any of the chosen few "sight holders" wanting to buy rough stones can do so only at the De Beers's periodic "sights," in London.

The "sights" are one of the most fascinating aspects of the diamond world, and they give a good indication of the importance of De Beers. Unlike most commodities, diamonds are not simply put up for sale on the open market and allowed to reach their market price. Approximately 85 percent of the diamonds that ultimately find their way into jewelry or into a collector's vault pass from the producer to the consumer through the hands of a De Beers subsidiary called the Central Selling Organization, or CSO. It is the CSO, not the free market, which effectively sets the price of the gemstones.

It does so ten times a year, in a house on London's Charterhouse Street owned by the Diamond Trading Company—another De Beers subsidiary. In this house, diamond dealers from all over the world gather to inspect the latest crop of rough stones in a ceremony known as a "sight." In order to be invited to a sight, you have to have an ironclad reputation, a steady business and the willingness to purchase a presorted, preselected lot of diamonds on the CSO's say-so, not your own. The organization attempts to give its clients selections reflecting their individual needs, but there are no precise "orders" given, and the CSO's decision is final. The house on Charterhouse Street is truly a seller's market.

Think about this for a minute. Imagine you are a buyer of rough diamonds and you have just been invited to one of the CSO's ten-yearly sights. You walk into a huge room with several hundred other buyers and sit down at a long table to await the viewing of your gems. You have already told the CSO how many one-carat diamonds you would like, how many large stones, how many "melees" (very small stones), etc., and you have based this request on your current manufacturing requirements. After a short wait, your stones arrive. You open the box of gems eagerly, to see what the organization has selected for you. Perhaps all goes well: perhaps the organization's own marketing requirements have coincided with yours, you find the "asking" price fair and you sign over your check for the lot. But what if something goes wrong? What if they have given you twice as much in small stones as you can use? What if you find a fracture in one of the stones, or you find the price of the middle-range roughs much higher than you had expected? What recourse do you have?

The strange, but accurate, answer is . . . none at all. In a very few cases, the CSO will agree to exchange a diamond that is obviously flawed or improperly priced, but in the great majority of sights, you must buy your whole box without complaining—or be barred from future sights. There is no picking and choosing on Charterhouse Street: when the CSO hands you your box, it's take it all or leave it. And at the price the organization demands.

Imagine this kind of control being levied against the customer in any other line of business. Imagine a farmer walking into a feedstore and being told which grain to buy and which price he will have to pay. Imagine a tire manufacturer going to U.S. Rubber and being told, "You can have precisely this many tons of precisely this grade of rubber, and you will pay us precisely this amount." The idea is unthinkable—yet it is standard operating procedure in the diamond rough business.

You can get some idea of the power of the CSO by hearing the terms applied to it by people in the diamond business. Probably the most common term—and it is a term that is applied to De Beers at large as well as to its selling arm, the CSO—is "the Syndicate." If this term evokes images of a vast omnipotent combine that makes offers that cannot be refused, that evocation is not accidental. The word Syndicate actually grew out of the title of Cecil Rhodes's selling arm, the London-based Diamond Syndicate, but it is entirely fitting that it suggests widespread power as well.

Other, less common terms also suggest the organization's omnipotence. Murray Schumach, in his entertaining book *The Diamond People,* says that De Beers's vast funds make it almost a "separate government." The not entirely generous Edward Jay Epstein, in his article "Have You Ever Tried to Sell a Diamond?" calls it "the most successful cartel arrangement in the annals of modern commerce." Monty Charles, the powerful head of the Diamond Trading Company, speaking to Timothy Green, calls his organization "a benevolent monopoly" (see *The World of Diamonds).*

You might suppose that, faced with an organization of such tremendous power as De Beers, many people would resent and argue against its control. Surprisingly, this is not a widespread reaction. In the world of diamonds, even staunch free traders become convinced of the virtues of central planning. Outsiders such as Epstein have objected that De

Beers's unified control of all levels of diamond marketing has had the effect of artificially raising prices and perpetuating what he calls "the illusion of scarcity."[1] Few people in the diamond business would agree with him, and for obvious reasons. While it may rankle a liberal mind to see any commodity price controlled, it is quite clear—at least to those in the industry—that on balance De Beers's "supervision" of the diamond world has had more good than ill effects.

This is important to remember if you are considering investing in diamonds. If you are a potential novice investor, one of the most salubrious aspects of diamond history in this century is that the price of these remarkable gems has risen slowly but steadily in spite of wars, economic disasters and other features of twentieth-century life that tend to destabilize the prices of other commodities. With the exception of the investment-diamond explosion of the late 1970s (about which we'll talk in Chapter 9), the gems have maintained their price stability pretty well throughout the entire century, and it is certainly not stretching a point to say that much of the reason for this remarkable steady appreciation in value is the strict, "benevolent" control of De Beers.

It's not only investors that appreciate the strong hand of the South African monopoly. In spite of Epstein's reservations—and I do not say they are all wrong—most major buyers of diamonds are quite content with the way the system operates. They may resent De Beers and the Syndicate privately, but in public it's another story. So central is the CSO to the entire marketing of the gems that, no matter how stringent its requirements and no matter how little leeway it gives its sight holders, there are always dealers straining to get in. To be accorded a CSO sight is still what Timothy Green calls "the ultimate accolade in the diamond trade," and there are few who would pass it up, whatever their private views of the Syndicate.

Up to now, I have been speaking only of *rough* stones. All the stones that are put out on those tables in Charterhouse Street are newly mined, uncut diamonds. They have been selected and sorted more or less according to what the individual sight holders have indicated they want, and since those sight holders are all involved in the gem trade (rather than in the industrial use of diamonds), the stones on view are of various quality but all gem-worthy items. But they are not the finished product. To transform a newly mined diamond from a rough to a finished stone, the sight holders put it through a necessary production step, one that takes place generally in New York, Antwerp, Tel Aviv or

[1] Epstein, "Have You Ever Tried to Sell a Diamond?" p. 23.

Bombay. This step is the manufacturing, or cutting, step—and it is this step that releases the gem-quality diamond's true value and beauty.

FROM ROUGH STONE TO GEMSTONE

The diamond that Erasmus Jacobs picked up on the bank of the Orange River did not look very much like the diamond in your engagement ring, and indeed rough diamonds in general do not possess nearly the sparkle and brilliance that we associate with the precious stones. In their rough state, diamonds are vaguely shiny, somewhat opaque stones often with an oily surface and with colors that range from a light, off-white yellow to black. If your idea of diamonds were limited to what you have seen set into jewelry, you might easily mistake a good rough for just another piece of dull quartz.

Most rough diamonds, moreover, never make it into jewelry at all. The vast majority of today's diamond production goes into neither investment nor adornment, but into industry. Because of the diamond's extreme hardness, it has long been considered important in industries in which an infinitely sharp "blade" is essential to manufacture: diamonds are used to cut not only other diamonds, but also various types of stone and bedrock. Oil drill bits are studded with diamonds, stonemasons rely on diamond saws, and even surgeons depend on diamond scalpels for their finest, most delicate incisions. Because of their high melting point, diamonds are also used in spacecraft for parts that must endure extreme temperatures: the window through which NASA cameras photographed Venus on the 1978 probe flight was constructed of a single large diamond.

Of the diamonds produced today, over 80 percent find their way into industrial applications. That's over 100 million carats of rough stones a year, most of which are used as diamond "grit" or "dust" to provide the cutting edges for industrial tools. Only the remaining 20 percent of production ends up being turned into gemstones—and less than 1 percent of the total is considered fine enough in quality to qualify as investment-level material.

But it is that 20 percent of mined stones that accounts for the bulk of De Beers's profit and sustains in the popular mind the image of diamonds as matchless gems. It is that 20 percent that ends up on the tables at Charterhouse Street and finds its way ultimately into your ring. It is for these stones that people pay upwards of 10 or 20 thousand dollars a carat—a price that would be unthinkable for an industrial-quality stone.

There is a reason that this 20 percent of diamonds is considered so much more valuable, in terms of price per carat, than the industrial 80 percent. It is that these stones, before they reach your local jeweler, pass through a manufacturing process that transforms them, in Murray Schumach's words, from "unappealing bits of grayish carbon into the brilliant diamonds calculated to attract large amounts of money in the name of love, sentiment, or investment."[2] That process is the finishing, or cutting, process; without it, diamonds would be just so much hard crystal.

The diamond cutter's art is an old and highly respected one in the industry, for everyone connected with diamonds understands that, without the cutter, no diamond would possess the peculiar optical brilliance that makes these stones so desirable. The business of the cutter is to refashion nature's work so that the inherent reflective capabilities of the stone will show to best advantage—to release what diamond people call the stone's inner *fire* (the dispersion of white light into spectral color) and *brilliance* (the white light reflected to the viewer). To do so, he employs four major techniques:

1. Cleaving

Diamonds are crystals, and their carbon atoms are arranged in a generally predictable internal pattern: an octohedral lattice structure displaying certain lines of strength and certain other lines of stress. The first thing that a diamond cutter has to do, when he receives a large rough stone, is to break it down into smaller, more workable fragments; the oldest method of doing this is by cleaving. When a cutter cleaves a diamond, he cuts a small groove, called a *kerf,* in the rough stone, places a steel blade in the groove, and taps it lightly with a mallet. If he has judged the angles of the stone correctly, it will split neatly along its internal lines of least resistance, and he will have two or more small pieces, which can then be further worked.

If he judges the angles improperly, however, the result can be disaster. The diamond, if it is not hit exactly right, can shatter in a hundred pieces, none of them large enough to be worthwhile for gem work. That is why the cleaver's art has been called "high drama." Everyone in the diamond trade knows the story of certain famous cleavings—and everyone, too, can tell of certain fabulous failures. The tale of how Lazare Kaplan cleaved the famous Jonker diamond in 1936, for example, is told among diamond people like a kind of ancient family legend. Kaplan, the most celebrated cleaver of this century, studied the potential lines of cleavage of this huge stone for nearly a year before bringing out his mallet. Almost as popular is the story of Joseph Asscher, who after cleaving the Cullinan diamond (the largest diamond ever found) had to be hospitalized for several weeks to get over the accumulated tension.

2. Sawing

Cleaving takes place along the lines of least internal resistance, or—as diamond cutters say—"with the grain" of the stone. Sawing, on the other hand, takes place "against the grain." It is a much slower process than cleaving, and also a much less risky one. It is much more common than cleaving, and even stones that have been cleaved will generally be further broken down by sawing.

Sawing a diamond, in spite of the similarity in terminology, is not like sawing a piece of wood. Both substances are cut against the grain, but there the similarity stops. When a diamond is sawed, it is first placed in a device to hold it steady (a "dop"), and then it is lowered very carefully onto the edge of a steel disk, revolving at 1,700 rpm, whose edges have been rubbed with a mixture of diamond dust and oil. The dust acts as the cutting abrasive, and the oil keeps the dust in place.

Sawing through a diamond with one of these rotary blades may take as little as several hours or as much as several days. The speed of the operation depends partly on the size of the diamond and also on the tension that is created when the blade meets an included crystal or a "knot" (a change of grain direction) in the stone. In spite of their hardness, diamonds can break apart if they are jarred too harshly or for too long a time by a whirring blade. So the person operating the diamond saw has to be attentive to strain in the structure of the stone and be ready to halt or slow down the process if the tension becomes too great.

Often, when a diamond cutter suspects that the internal stresses are endangering the stone, he will place it under a polariscope. The presence of a "rainbow effect" in a stone seen under this sensitive instrument may indicate internal strain and force the cutter to use extra care. This is a rare problem, however—and it is obviously less potentially disastrous than the all-or-nothing hazards of cleaving.

3. Faceting

I have been speaking of "cutters" as if they performed all kinds of manufacturing processes on their stones. This is true when you think of a cutter in the generic sense of being anybody who works physically on diamonds. There is a narrower definition of "cutter," however, and that is the one I'll use here. Within the world of diamond workers, a cutter is often considered to be only the person who does the faceting of the finished stone; "cutting" in this sense is often used as a synonym for "faceting."

A "facet" in a diamond is one of the many external planes that are polished on it for the purpose of enhancing its optical properties. Without facets, diamonds would still sparkle modestly, but they would have little of the scintillation that makes them such attractive investments. The cutter who concentrates on faceting is the person who ultimately is responsible for the way the diamond looks to you, and if he does his job properly, you will get a diamond of exceptional optical properties.

Faceting can be a long and arduous process, and although shortcuts abound in this field as in any other, the finest diamonds are faceted by professionals who appreciate that the gem's final appearance is largely their responsibility. Diamond cutters know precisely how large or small each of the facets should be for maximum brilliance, precisely what angles they should bear to each other, and precisely how many of them a given stone needs to become all it is capable of becoming.

We will talk more about the art of faceting—and about its exact mathematical nature—in the following chapter. Here you should keep in mind that a good faceter can make the difference between an indifferent stone and one of extraordinary beauty. The faceter is like a sculptor in miniature: his job is—as Michelangelo is supposed to have said about his own job on the "David"—to remove the excess material so that the perfect form lying within the stone can be revealed to view. Since a standard diamond today has fifty-eight distinct facets (that is the number that has been found to create the most brilliant gem), it is obvious that the cutter's job is a meticulous and demanding one.

"Removing the excess material" of a diamond has the same effect as removing the excess marble of the "David." It reduces the weight of the stone, because in faceting, as in other cutting procedures, a certain amount of rough stone is inevitably lost. This doesn't necessarily mean a loss in value, for a rough stone, just like a piece of uncut marble, always has a certain value. However, it is never certain, no matter how valuable the rough, what the final value of the finished product will be. Only if the cutter is very lucky will he get a finished gem of the finest color and brilliance.

Most finely faceted stones are about half or a little more than half the weight, in carats, of the rough stones from which they are "carved." To some cutters, this is a constant annoyance, and the more weight-conscious among them sometimes try to cut corners for the purpose of saving weight—that is, they give a stone improperly aligned facets, because that will make the final gem heavier than a properly cut one would be. The reason for this improper cutting, or "swindling," is to maintain a more salable weight. For example, a proper cut on a given rough might yield a .95-carat, or 95-point, stone, while a swindle cut would yield the less attractive but more marketable full carat.

Swindle cutting is doing more than robbing Peter to pay Paul. It is perverting the very notion of the cutter's art. Lazare Kaplan is fond of pointing out that a diamond worker who goes for weight, rather than fineness of cut, is like a butcher who leaves too much fat on a cut of meat. "The steak weighs more" that way, he says, "but it's not as valuable."[3] This is a sound observation. If you are concerned that a faceter, in creating a brilliant gem, inevitably "wastes" some of the rough stone, you might just as well chide Michelangelo for "wasting" so much of his marble: the obvious, and absurd, conclusion to this line of thinking is that the famous statue would have been much "better"— much more "valuable," in any case—if the sculptor had given it a pot belly or a couple of extra hands.

4. Polishing

Polishing is the final step in the diamond cutter's work. There is nothing very mysterious about this step. All it means is that the cutter takes the finished gem and polishes off its surface irregularities by grinding them down on a wheel. This creates, like the other steps, a more beautiful gem, since it enhances the optical properties. Polishing is the finishing touch.

These are the basic four processes that professional cutters use to bring out the best in their gems. When a diamond has gone through these steps, it is ready for its next—and final—stop: it is ready to be inspected, admired and (one hopes) purchased by you as an adornment or an investment.

BUYING THE FINISHED PRODUCT

Each segment of a diamond's "life" is associated, generally, with a particular part of the world. One of the fascinating aspects of diamond trading is the international element involved. The newly mined diamonds, as we've seen, still come largely from South Africa, although in recent years industrial-quality diamonds have been coming from a variety of other places as well. Among the other countries that now supply diamonds to the world market are—in order of decreasing importance —Zaire, the Soviet Union, Botswana, Ghana, Sierra Leone, Namibia,

[3] Quoted in Green, *The World of Diamonds,* p. 213.

Venezuela and Brazil. Numerous other nations, most of them in Africa, also supply some gems.

The center of the marketing step—for both industrial-quality and gem diamonds—is the CSO offices in London, although other diamond "bourses" operate in such trading centers as Antwerp, Tel Aviv, Bombay, Amsterdam and New York.

For the cutting step, there are several homes. The oldest and still among the most productive is Antwerp, where Jewish craftsmen have been cutting since the Middle Ages. Next in importance to Antwerp are Tel Aviv, home of the Israeli industry; New York, where most large diamonds are cut; the Indian cities of Bombay and Surat; Johannesburg; Hong Kong, and Amsterdam. (Amsterdam, once the center of the cutter's art, has never fully recovered from the Nazi extermination of Dutch Jews.)

Once a diamond passes out of one of these centers, it goes to one of a variety of retail centers around the world. In New York, where I work and where the vast bulk of U.S. diamonds are traded, these centers may be as elegant and exclusive as Harry Winston's famous Fifth Avenue shop, or as geared to the man in the street as the many shops that line 47th Street ("The Street," as diamond people call it) between Fifth Avenue and the Avenue of the Americas. It is in these retail centers that you will most likely come across diamonds that you might want to purchase.

I say "might" because I realize that there is today a great deal of uncertainty and even fear in the realm of diamond purchasing. Since the huge rush to buy investment stones has quieted down considerably since 1980, I am often asked whether or not these sparklers are still good investments. It's perfectly apparent that diamonds are useful to industry, and that they are beautiful objects in their own right. But does that mean you should rush out and buy them?

There is a great deal of disagreement in the industry today about whether or not diamonds are a good "investment." Opinions differ widely, and they range from those of the radical optimists, who say that the gems are bound to multiply tenfold in value before the end of the decade, to those of the extreme pessimists, such as Edward Jay Epstein, who claims that it is impossible to resell a fine diamond today, because the De Beers policy of pushing all its stones into jewelry makes resale too difficult.[4]

Probably the truth of the matter lies somewhere between these extreme views. With the wisdom of hindsight it now seems obvious that

[4] Epstein, op. cit.

the investment-diamond explosion of 1979–80 escalated the price of the gems to unreasonably high levels and that you cannot hope to get in on the ground floor of that boom any longer: indeed, many of the latecomers into the boom are now stuck with diamonds that they bought for $55,000 a carat and that they can resell for only $15,000 to $20,000 a carat. To that extent, the pessimists are right: it is simply too late now to cash in on the speculative fortunes that were made (and lost) in the wild days of 1979–80.

On the other hand, the optimists point out, diamonds have proved remarkably resistant to serious price fluctuations for many hundreds of years, and there are good reasons for believing that they will continue to do so. The investment-diamond madness, they claim, was a unique and short-lived phenomenon—and in spite of the fact that some speculators did lose money in it, the market was ultimately regulated: the De Beers umbrella proved waterproof. Current per-carat prices, the optimistic say, are more truly reflective of the actual value of the gems—which means that investing now is a relatively safe venture.

There is a sound basis to this line of thinking; it's encouraging for a potential investor to be reminded that the per-carat appreciation of high-quality diamonds has been extremely steady for many years, and that a stone that you bought in 1970 for one thousand dollars could have fetched $32,000 in 1981. Since then, of course, the price has come down—but not so much that buying a diamond in 1970 would not still have been a very good move.

Of course, you are not in the position today of being able to buy a diamond at 1970 prices, but even so I generally agree with current optimism. Diamonds, in spite of the recent price fluctuations, have proved to be quite reliable investments throughout this turbulent century. Aside from the fact that they are widely admired for their beauty, they have also been acquired, with good results, because of their scarcity, their portability, their liquidity, their freedom from government control, and of course their durability. Many people have purchased them as a hedge against inflation, and this has proved a wise course of action in many cases, since their average rate of appreciation has always more than kept pace with inflation. So, even though this is not as prime a time for investment diamonds as 1970 or 1920, it is not really a bad time either.

If you are going to buy diamonds, however, there are a few things you need to know before you enter a shop. Largely because of the investment-diamond craze, buying diamonds today is a far more complicated procedure than it was even ten years ago. If you are not to be deluded into purchasing relatively worthless stones, you need to familiarize yourself first with how diamonds are graded and valued.

CHAPTER 8

THE FOUR C's

In 1812, the Austrian mineralogist Friedrich Mohs proposed a numerical scale to measure the relative hardness of minerals. He took talc to be among the softest of minerals and assigned it the scale value of 1. He then arranged nine other minerals at points of increasing hardness along the scale, with gypsum being placed at 2, quartz at 7 and diamond at 10. Setting diamond at the far end of the hardness scale was Mohs's way of acknowledging what geologists and gemologists had known for centuries: that the diamond was the hardest substance in nature.

It is important to remember that "hardness" here does not mean "invincibility." It does not mean that a diamond cannot be cracked or shattered by a blow; diamonds are hard, but brittle. If you punch a brick wall with a diamond ring on your finger, you may well chip or crack the gem, even though the brick is softer. You will not, however, *scratch* its surface. A diamond, as Mohs pointed out, can be scratched only by another diamond. That is the meaning of his scale: it identifies which minerals will scratch, or cut, other minerals. Each mineral will scratch minerals of the same or a lower number, and will be unable to scratch any of a higher number.

This fact has had enormous consequences for industry. Because nothing can scratch a diamond but another diamond, and because a diamond can cut anything else with relative ease, it has been widely used as a "blade" in industrial applications. The rotary bits that dig through thousands of feet of bedrock to find new oil supplies are studded with diamonds. High-quality glass-cutting knives are made of diamond. Diamond powder, or "dust," is used to make a variety of industrial abrasives. And diamond dies are used to cut extremely fine metal wire. All of this in addition, of course, to the crystal's many uses in the gem trade, where the old phrase "Only a diamond will cut diamond" is taken literally every day.

But is it the diamond's hardness, ultimately, that makes it so valuable on the world market? Since over 80 percent of the rough diamonds mined these days are used uncut by industry, may hardness reasonably be taken as the diamond's most marketable property—whether it is being set into an engagement ring or imbedded in an oil-drilling bit?

Not really. Even though the great majority of diamonds never find their way into jewelry, it is the small percentage that does that ultimately determines the crystal's market price. These stones—the "top of the line" of world production—are no harder than the stones being used in drill bits, but they possess a quality that the drill-bit stones don't have, and this quality has for centuries given diamonds a value far above their potential value to industry. I am speaking, of course, of their beauty.

Beauty is a relative quality, naturally, and there is much truth in the proposition that it resides in the eye of the beholder. No doubt there are cultures somewhere on the planet that would regard a diamond as nothing but another shiny stone, and would take gypsum, or opal, or wood chips, as the ultimate criterion of beauty. But these cultures need not concern us here, for it is a matter of historical record that in virtually all modern societies, diamonds have been regarded—and continue to be regarded—as objects of remarkable aesthetic appeal. Today, thanks to the century-long marketing of De Beers, the "sparklers" are almost universally respected as adornment—and it is because of this, and not the stone's great hardness, that diamonds can be a good investment.

When you purchase diamonds, you will not be buying the large, uncut "roughs" that are used to cut through rock and metal in industry. You will be buying the top of the line: the carefully cut, polished stones that generally find their way into jewelry and that, in the past several years, have increasingly found their way, as "loose" diamonds, into safety-deposit boxes.

When you buy diamonds like these, you will have to concern yourself with more than the stones' peculiar hardness—and even with more than their obvious aesthetic appeal. Remember, *all* diamonds are hard, so if you were buying them simply on that basis, one stone would be as good as another. In addition, all diamonds possess a certain basic aesthetic appeal, even in a "rough" condition—so you might easily think that, as long as the stone appeals to you, you would be safe in making the investment.

Thinking that way would get you into serious trouble in today's diamond market. Not only are today's stones not all alike, but the distinctions drawn between quite similar stones are of an infinite fineness. What I will do in this chapter is to give you the basic working terminology that you will need to judge diamonds intelligently, *before* you commit your money. What you need is the vocabulary of diamond trading: the vocabulary that all professional traders use among themselves in weighing the merits of diamonds. If you learn this vocabulary before you shop around, you will be in a better position to speak sensibly about your prospective purchase to an honest seller—and to spot the chicanery of a dishonest one.

The vocabulary of diamonds is a little more complex than that of gold or silver, but there are really only four terms that are absolutely essential for you to understand. Conveniently, all four of these terms begin with the same letter. People who deal in diamonds regularly call them the trade's "four C's." They are *carat, color, clarity* and *cut.*

THE FIRST C: CARAT

You'll notice first of all that both diamonds and gold are measured according to *carats (karats).* That is because in ancient times both were weighed against the carob bean, which is *qirat* in Arabic, and the outmoded, but colorful, designation has stuck. To avoid confusion, the word is spelled with a "c" when applied to diamonds, and a "k" when applied to gold. This orthographic distinction is the sign of an important difference: the fact that karat in gold is a measure of *purity,* and carat in diamonds is a measure of *weight.*

In Chaper 2 I noted that pure, or virtually 100 percent, gold was designated 24-karat gold. That is, a single karat of gold referred simply to a twenty-fourth part of complete purity. You can have a one-ounce wafer of 24-karat gold, a 24-ounce chunk of 24-karat gold or a one-kilo bar of 24-karat gold. The term "karat" has nothing to do with weight.

In diamonds, on the other hand, it has everything to do with weight and nothing to do with purity. Carat weight in diamonds is simply that and nothing more: a measure of how much the diamond weighs. A carat of weight is defined as one fifth of a gram, or 200 milligrams. This is an exact designation, and when people buy and sell diamonds, they determine the stones' carat weight by using extremely sensitive balance scales. Weights are sometimes estimated by measuring a stone's size against a precut template, but this is an approximate and not very reliable method of measurement. If you are thinking of buying a stone, the first thing you should determine is how much it weighs in carats according to a reliable jeweler's scale.

Carat weight is seen by some as an old-fashioned system which needs replacing, and as a result some dealers will quote you a weight in the *point* system instead. There is nothing superior about this system, but there is nothing wrong with it either, and it does have the advantage of making it a little easier to measure small or fractional-carat stones. A

THE FOUR C'S   119

point is simply one hundredth of a carat, or 2 milligrams. A one-carat stone, therefore, weighs 100 points. You should be aware of this "refinement" of the diamond measurement system, because a jeweler or a dealer may describe a stone as being, say, 151 points in weight. All this means is that it is one carat plus 51 points—or one point over one and a half carats.

Even that one point might make a difference, though, so you should not disregard point weights. No honest dealer, for example, will sell you a 95-point diamond and tell you that it weighs "approximately" one carat. It does weigh approximately one carat, but the 5-point difference in weight could mean a 30 percent difference in value.

Two further facts should be mentioned about carat weight, since they are frequently misunderstood by the amateur:

First, there is a significant difference in weight between a stone that has just been mined—a "rough" diamond—and one that has subsequently been cut and polished. The cutting and polishing process is an essential one for gem-quality diamonds, but it is one that extracts a large toll. Most experienced cutters consider themselves fortunate if they can "save" 50 or 60 percent of a rough stone in the final cut one; many stones lose over 50 percent of their weight in cutting. The smaller stones, of course, are much more valuable than the larger rough was, precisely because they have been cut. It is safe to say that finished diamonds are worth 25 percent more than the rough, with cutting costs accounting for about 1 to 10 percent of the total value.

Unless you are in the market for drill-bit studs, you will be buying cut diamonds. A fine cut diamond is no longer the gamble that the rough is, because with a cut diamond you know all the four C's. Just be aware that there is always a difference in weight between these diamonds and the roughs from which they have come.

The second point to remember is that, when you are shopping for diamonds, bigger is not necessarily better. This is commonly forgotten. Many people, raised on stories of the fabulous diamonds of the past, assume that the larger the stone, the more valuable it will be. Often they further assume that, with a given amount of money to spend, they will be much better off purchasing one huge "rock" than investing in several smaller ones. This is not necessarily the case.

Cut diamonds are now available in an enormous range of sizes, and if you are considering purchasing some, you should compare prices for various weights before you commit any money. A four carat diamond may look impressive on your finger, but you may encounter some difficulty when you decide to sell it years later. That is one drawback to buying big stones: their liquidity is not generally as good as that of the smaller variety—as Elizabeth Taylor discovered when, after their divorce, she tried to sell the mammoth, 69-carat diamond that Richard Burton had given her.

Generally speaking, it is much wiser to concentrate on one-carat diamonds than on either the monster variety or the smaller, cheaper stones. The one-carat diamond is a benchmark in the industry. Although many more smaller stones are bought and sold, the one-carat is still probably the best value for your money. The price of diamonds goes up disproportionately with carat size, and the one-carat is a reasonable balance, in terms of price per carat, between the quarter- or half-carat stones and the Taylor-Burton giants.

Another reason for being wary of the larger stones is that, in terms of ultimate value, carat weight may actually be the least important of the four C's. This may come as a surprise to you, since most Americans are impressed by size and since so many of us were raised to believe that the bigger the rock, the more expensive. Carat weight, indeed, is often taken as the single most important fact about a given diamond. Among diamond people, exactly the opposite is the case. If you ask a diamond professional to quote you a price on a one-carat stone, she will look at you blankly, because the value of gem diamonds has much less to do with carat weight than with the other three C's. "What kind of a one-carat diamond?" she will ask. Meaning, what color, what clarity, what cut?

THE SECOND C: COLOR

At the height of the investment-diamond craze, a woman called my office to say that she had a one-carat "blue-white perfect" diamond she wanted to sell; would I look at it? I knew that the chances of its really being blue-white and flawless were about as good as those of the Mets winning that year's pennant race, but I asked her to come in anyway.

As I had suspected, the diamond was not blue-white. By "blue-white" she had meant, and all diamond dealers mean too, a stone with no "body color" whatsoever—in other words, a completely colorless diamond with a very slight blue overtone. Such diamonds are extremely rare, and consequently very valuable. If the woman had actually had a one-carat blue-white flawless diamond, it might have been worth $65,000.

What she had, as I told her after examining the stone under my loupe, was a stone with a distinct yellowish tint that, at current prices, was worth about two thousand dollars. Not a bad price for a one-carat stone, but a far cry from what she had expected. Whoever had told her that she had a "blue-white" had relied on the common confusion among nonprofessionals about color, and colorlessness, in diamonds. Even among honest dealers, color terminology is so varied and contradictory that it is no surprise that the uneducated often are cheated by dealers who use this confusion to their benefit.

In nature, very few diamonds are completely colorless. Generally speaking, the less internal body color a diamond has, the more valuable it will be. For this reason, the rarer, colorless stones are the most valuable of all. "Blue-white" is a term that has been used for many years to identify completely colorless stones that, because of a peculiar fluorescent quality, appear to have a faint bluish hue. True blue-whites, however, are almost never seen in the market today, and the Gemological Institute of America, in its *Diamond Dictionary,* acknowledges that "Flagrant misuse has made the term meaningless."[1]

Most diamonds have a slight yellowish tint that is imparted to them in nature by the presence of slight impurities in the carbon crystal. As I've noted, diamonds are merely a compressed form of carbon, and it is their unique carbon bonding that gives them both their hardness and their beauty. Few diamonds, however, are composed of 100 percent-pure carbon, and because of the presence of noncarbon elements—geologists call them "allochromatics"—most diamonds are slightly "off-white": that is, they reflect not only white light, but other lights as well. The less yellow or other light they reflect, the more valuable they are.

Diamond professionals grade the color of their wares according to various color scales, and it is because there are so many of these scales that confusion still reigns in the matter of the "second C." If you will look at the chart on page 122, you will see that, even among utterly honest dealers, the range of colors that are assigned to diamonds is great, and the terms used to describe this range almost as great. The technique of color grading is further complicated by the fact that grading is subjective: what one person sees as an "F" stone, another may see as an "H." This can make for an appreciable difference in price—as much as $5,000 per carat between an "F" and an "H."

As a way of overcoming the dual confusions of subjectivity and diversity of grading systems, the diamond industry, in 1978, adopted what, it was hoped, would become a uniform color-grading scheme for all diamonds. If this scheme is widely adopted, it should clear up some of the current confusion. However, as of the printing of this book, the most widely accepted grading system worldwide is still that of the GIA.

[1] Robert Gaal, ed., *The Diamond Dictionary,* 2nd ed.

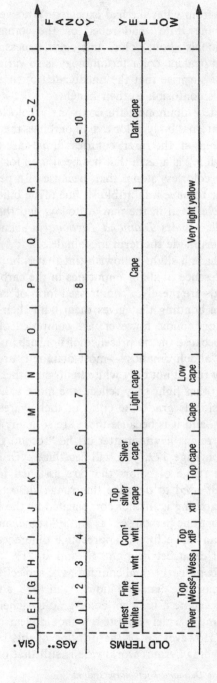

COMPARISON OF VARIOUS COLOR-GRADING SYSTEMS

GIA*	D	E	F	G	H	I	J	K	L	M	N	O	P	Q	R	S – Z

AGS**	0	1	2	3	4	5	6	7	8	9 – 10

OLD TERMS

Finest white	Fine wht	Com¹ wht	Top silver cape	Silver cape	Light cape	Cape	Dark cape

Top River	Wess²	Top Wess	Top xtl³	xtl	Top cape	Cape	Low cape	Very light yellow

FANCY

YELLOW

* Gemological Institute of America
** American Gem Society

1 Commercial
2 Wesselton
3 Crystal

The new international scale will become truly nonsubjective, more-over, only if people involved with diamonds have a clear-cut, standard-ized color scheme to eliminate subjectivity. This is what the GIA is trying to accomplish by its use of "master sets" of stones. These sets have been in existence for twenty-five years or so, but have become important only in the past ten years. Each master set, which can be purchased from the GIA, contains a series of GIA-graded diamonds against which a dealer or a prospective buyer can compare his or her own diamonds, and thus be assured of a standardized grade. A typical set might contain five half-carat stones: E, F, G, H and I. That would give the dealer a reliable standard against which to measure all stones of investment quality.

Since a master set of GIA-graded stones can be quite expensive, some dealers have chosen the option of buying color-grading sets made not of diamonds, but of "fake" diamonds such as cubic zirconia. These CZ sets, while they are not as accurate as diamond sets for purposes of color grading, are better than no set at all and will no doubt catch on in the industry: they are certainly much cheaper to buy.

What color stones should you buy? That will depend, of course, on how much you want to spend—but also on how eager you are to have a colorless, or close to colorless, stone. Many people are not particularly attracted to entirely colorless stones, and prefer to pay much less for a good "G" diamond than to go for broke and have an "E" or a "D" whose appearance they don't like any better. In terms of pure invest-ment principles, D-color stones are the best—but they are certainly not the only good buys, and as I've noted they are extremely expensive. If you stick to stones of at least a G or H color, you should be pretty well protected in terms of their ultimate resale value. I would not advise buying stones of a lower grade than K, because although they may be extremely attractive as jewelry stones, their inherent value as diamonds is much less than the value of a stone in the D to H range. The basic principle remains: other things being equal, the less color a stone has, the more valuable it will be.

But there is one major exception: fancy colors. If a stone has just a shade of yellow tinting, it is classed as "slightly tinted" or "tinted," and priced much lower than a colorless one. But if it has *enough* color, the price begins to rise again. If the stone is *obviously* colored, to the naked eye, it is no longer a mere tinted stone but can be what diamond people call a "fancy" stone. "Fancies" come in a variety of shades, including pink, red, orange, green, gold and blue (real blue, not "blue-white"). Some of the most valued diamonds of all time fall into this exceptional category.

The famous Hope diamond, for example, now in the Smithsonian Institution, in Washington, is a fabulous blue. The 129-carat Tiffany diamond, once owned by Charles Tiffany himself, is a yellow stone. And the pear-shaped Condé, which was owned by France's Louis XIII, is a lustrous pink.

The market for such fancies is perhaps not as predictable as the market for white or near-white stones, but if a stone has a distinct, obvious tint (and assuming it is a diamond), do not be frightened away just because you know that color means a decrease in value. For some collectors of diamonds, color is a positive asset—so much so, in fact, that numerous technical processes have been developed to artificially color stones that otherwise would have been merely a drab brownish or yellow hue. For those who fancy "fancies" at unfancy prices, even the artificial enhancement of a diamond's color is enough to increase its desirability.

Artificially enhanced stones, however, are never as valuable as natural stones of the same hue. Various radiation techniques are now employed to darken potentially desirable diamonds, and even though such processes do increase their worth, they are still somewhat stigmatized by being known as "treated" diamonds. The purists among diamond collectors will have nothing to do with them; for others, they represent an opportunity to buy a beautiful artificially colored "fancy" for a fraction of the price one might expect to pay for a naturally occurring tinted diamond.

Finally, it must be noted that the wide variety in color grades, the large increments in value that come from "jumping" or "dropping" a grade, and the peculiar "fancy" market have all led to chicanery and "colorful" disguises. Since color is so important in diamonds, it is no surprise that the unscrupulous have imparted to many diamonds shades that nature never intended—and passed them off as natural. More about this in Chapter 9.

THE THIRD C: CLARITY

When the carbon molecules that make up diamonds were "cooking" deep beneath the earth's surface millions of years ago, they were mixed with various noncarbon materials, and as noted in the previous section, those materials, when the carbon crystallized, often imparted color to the diamonds. But that is not all they imparted. In many cases, the "cooking" process was so turbulent that small particles of carbon or noncarbon material were trapped within the diamond, and these parti-

cles, called "inclusions," are seen in many of the diamonds mined today.

In addition, the crystallization process itself was seldom absolutely
"clean." In very few cases did the diamond form in a completely sym-
metrical, spot-free state: even diamonds which do not have trapped
hydrogen or carbon specks or resin in them contain imperfections in the
crystal structure itself. These imperfections, like the trapped alien material, are also called inclusions.

As the editors of Diamonds: Myth, Magic, and Reality point out,
inclusions mean one thing to the geologist and quite another to the gem
dealer or jeweler. To the geologist, such an imperfection can be regarded as a sign of individuality—evidence that the diamond that contains it is unique. Diamonds with such imperfections are traded with
great frequency—since totally "perfect" diamonds are so rare—and in
the words of one of the book's contributors, gemologist Eduard Gübelin, "In a sense an inclusion increases the worth of a diamond by giving
it individuality, setting it apart from millions of others."[2]

To the gemologist, however, this reasoning is spurious, and as attractive as an imperfect diamond may seem to you, if you are going to be
buying diamonds for more than their individuality, you will have to rely
on the gemologist's, rather than the geologist's, bias. According to that
bias, any imperfection in a stone reduces its market value, and the
greater the imperfection—no matter how charming it may be to the
geologist—the more the reduction. In terms of the third C, clarity,
every little quirk of nature is that much more of a cut in the product's
selling price.

Clarity in diamonds, then, is equivalent to visual purity. When a
diamond seller speaks of a stone of "flawless clarity," he means one in
which no inclusions are visible, either to the naked eye or under ten-
power magnification. When he speaks of a stone as "imperfect" or
"clouded," on the other hand, he means one that nature has given one
or more of those interesting, but economically negative, inclusions.

There are various types of inclusions, and although they all reduce
the value of the diamond that contains them, they are not all equally
serious. Among those that you are most likely to come across are the
following:

■ Clouds. These are actually groups of tiny inclusions that,
grouped together, give an area of the diamond a cottony or opaque
appearance.

[2] Jacques Legrand, ed., Diamonds: Myth, Magic, and Reality, p. 222.

■ *Feathers.*   Minute cracks or cleavages within the diamond's internal structure.

■ *Included crystals.*   Crystals, either of diamond or of an alien mineral, within the larger diamond crystal. These are sometimes called "bubbles" or, when they are dark, "carbon spots."

■ *Knots.*   Included crystals that have broken through the surface of the diamond.

■ *Pinpoints.*   Tiny inclusions that look like white dots when seen under ten-power magnification.

All of these inclusions occur within the structure of the diamond: that's why they are called inclusions. Other irregularities occur on the surface of the diamond, and although these are less serious than inclusions, you should still be aware of them. Surface irregularities are called *blemishes.* The most common examples are the following:

■ *Abrasions.*   These are chips on the edges of a facet caused by two diamonds rubbing together. Abrasions are often called "paper marks," because they are a common result of diamonds being carried together in paper packets.

■ *Naturals.*   Portions of the original rough stone left on the surface of the polished diamond, often to prevent extra loss of weight when cutting.

■ *Percussion marks.*   Bruises caused by pointed objects. They are commonly surrounded by minute feathering cleavages.

■ *Pits.*   Surface indentations. The smaller ones are usually called nicks, the larger ones cavities.

■ *Scratches.*   Often caused by contact with other diamonds, they are also caused by contact with defective grinding wheels—in which case they are called "wheel marks."

One reason that both inclusions and blemishes are considered defects by the diamond collector is that a principal attraction of fine stones is their ability to reflect light, and the larger imperfections impair this reflective ability. Another reason is what might be called the allure of perfection. Diamonds are considered almost works of fine art: the serious collector would no more want to own a blemished or clouded diamond than he would want to own a Picasso with a tear in the corner. With diamonds, any deviations from the ultimate goal of perfection tend to reduce their value.

Blemishes can often be removed by further polishing or grinding. This would reduce the carat weight of the stone somewhat, but it might be worth the effort if it produced a finer specimen. Inclusions cannot be so removed, because they are within the stone.

So inclusions are almost always more serious than blemishes. But they are not all of an identical seriousness. Virtually all diamonds have some tiny imperfections: it is safe to say that there has never been a truly "perfect" diamond. But there have been many diamonds that have been called "loupe perfect" or "loupe clean" because they reveal no imperfections when viewed under a ten-power magnifying glass. The ten-power loupe is still the most common magnifying instrument used in the diamond trade, and a diamond that is clean under that magnification is considered a very fine specimen indeed. When imperfections are detected under that magnification, the next thing you have to find out is how serious they are. Gemologist E. Gübelin explains the basic principles involved in making that determination:

> Flaws that are visible under a 10× lens reduce the value of the diamond; just how much the value is reduced depends on the size and number of the inclusions, their influence on optical properties, their degree of visibility or position in the crystal, and their potential effect on the firmness (which may be weakened by fractures) of the diamond. Obviously, inclusions that are easily visible count more than those that are barely discernible, and colored mineral inclusions count more than inclusions of the same size that are colorless and transparent.[3]

But there is a further point to be made about inclusions that is a direct result of the recent surge of interest in investment diamonds. Up until a few years ago, a diamond that exhibited no imperfections under a ten-power lens was considered to be "flawless"—or "internally flawless" if it showed blemishes but no inclusions. "Flawless" remains the highest standard of clarity for diamonds, but due to the investment-diamond craze and increasing sophistication in magnification technology, far fewer diamonds receive that categorization today than would have ten years ago. Today, the ten-power loupe is only the beginning tool when it comes to the finest specimens. A stone that is apparently flawless is now often viewed under a ten-power microscope, and such viewing sometimes reveals flaws that the loupe didn't pick up.

The significance of this for the novice diamond buyer is that it is much more difficult today to find true flawless diamonds than it was ten years ago. I would estimate that, at any one time, there are no more than fifteen or twenty 1-carat D-flawless diamonds (diamonds of the highest color grade and the highest clarity grade) on the market: the rest are in safety-deposit vaults. Many diamonds that would have been given a "flawless" rating before the investment surge are now being classed as VVS₁ or even VVS₂. (See the following chart for the clarity grading system accepted by most of the diamond trade.) Ten years ago, Tiffany's top-of-the-line diamond—a one-carat River flawless specimen —sold for about $3,000. Today diamonds of that superior grade are so much more carefully investigated that probably not one in ten that used to be considered top grade still receives the D-flawless rating—and it now sells for $20,000 per carat.

Diamond Clarity Grading System

All examinations are done with ten-power loupe magnification. The following are *verbal* guidelines; within each category there are no strict parameters.

FLAWLESS

Diamond has no inclusions (internal imperfections) or surface blemishes.

* AGS equivalent	INTERNALLY FLAWLESS
0	Diamond has no inclusions and only minor surface blemishes, which can often be removed with polishing.
1 - 2	VVS₁ and VVS₂ (very very slight) VVS₁—Diamond generally has only a microscopic inclusion visible from the back of the stone. VVS₂—Diamond with a microscopic imperfection barely visible through the top of the stone.
3 - 4	VS₁ and VS₂ (very slight) VS₁—Stone is characterized by inclusions that are very difficult to see with a ten-power loupe. VS₂—Stone is characterized by inclusions that are somewhat difficult to see with a ten-power loupe.
5 - 6	SI₁ and SI₂ (slight) SI₁—Contains inclusions that are somewhat easy to see with a ten-power loupe. SI₂—Contains inclusions that are easy to see with a ten-power loupe but are usually not noticeable to the unaided eye.

I₁, I₂ and I₃ (imperfect)

I₁—Contains inclusions that are visible to the unaided eye.

7 - 8 - 9   I₂—Contains inclusions that are obvious to the unaided eye.

I₃—Industrial-quality diamond.

* American Gem Society

This means that, as a new diamond purchaser, you have to be very careful about clarity grades. Generally speaking, only diamonds that are at least an H color and VS₂ quality are worthwhile for investment purposes. Diamonds of a lower grade than that may be fine for ornamentation, and I certainly do not say you should not buy a diamond ring with a K/SI₂ diamond in it if you think it's attractive. But as an investment vehicle such a diamond is not the best bet.

To avoid getting taken on either carat, color or clarity, what you need as a buyer is official trade assurance that the diamond you are buying is a certain weight and grade. You get that assurance from the GIA, which issues a certificate describing in great detail each diamond investigated. I'll talk more about these absolutely essential certificates in the next chapter. Now let's look at the "fourth C", one that unfortunately is not so easily protected by certificate and yet is extremely important—sometimes more important than any of the other three—in determining a diamond's real value.

THE FOURTH C: CUT

In the previous chapter, I spoke about how rough diamonds are brought from Africa to Antwerp and New York, where they are fashioned into jewelry-worthy gems by those geniuses of the diamond world, the cutters. Sad to say, the work of these artisans—many of them belonging to the fourth or fifth generation of diamond-cutting families—is little appreciated by the general public. It is not going too far to say that without the efforts of skilled cutters, diamonds would be worth little more today than they were a hundred years ago. It is the advent of precision cutting in the past couple of generations that largely accounts for the fineness of today's gems. For that reason, the fourth C should receive much more attention than it generally is given.

The term "cut" is frequently used interchangeably with the term "proportions." When diamond people talk about "cut," they mean all those elements that contribute to the overall shape and geometry of the stone: the size of the individual facets, their relation to each other and so on. Each cutter may have his own peculiarities of style in fashioning a gem, but in general there are widely accepted theories among cutters as to what proportions are best for given diamond shapes; there are, in other words, "ideal" proportions for given gems.

On pages 132–33 you will see diagrams of some common contemporary diamond cuts. The first thing a cutter must do when he receives a rough stone is to determine which of these basic shapes the finished stone will be. (As a matter of fact, this is not always a cutter's decision, but one that is sometimes determined by market forces.) Once that has been decided, he must then determine which proportions of faceting will be most likely to release the "fire" and "brilliance" of that shape gem to best advantage. If he does his work properly, the diamond will be an attractive, brilliant specimen; if he does it poorly, it will be just another run-of-the-mill "sparkler."

If I am making it sound as if the cutter's decisions about proportions are a matter of personal whim, that is not the case. For many years now, there have been recognized "patterns" of cutting the various shapes, and while cutters may have their idiosyncracies, these patterns are pretty widely observed. This is because experience has demonstrated that, by using them, cutters can achieve the best and most consistent results.

Take, for an example, the proportions of the most popular of diamond cuts, the so-called round, or brilliant, cut. This is the familiar round cut with the tapered base that you find in most modern engagement rings.

The modern brilliant cut is the end result of years of experiment on proportions that were first laid down systematically in 1919 by the mathematician Marcel Tolkowsky. The "Tolkowsky theoretical brilliant cut" was designed for "maximum brilliancy consistent with a high degree of fire in a round diamond brilliant."[4] ("Brilliancy" refers to the white light reflected to the observer, "fire" to the play of inner light in the diamond.) Tolkowsky prescribed exact rules to achieve this optimum effect, and many cutters today still think of them as gospel: deviations from the Tolkowsky proportions, they claim, are deviations from the ideal. You can see these supposed ideal proportions on page 131.

As a matter of fact, however, not all diamonds today are cut in accordance with Tolkowsky's method. There are two reasons for this: One is that some cutters simply disagree with the "master" about which angles are best suited to achieve maximum fire and brilliance. The other is that, in the interests of saving carat weight, it is sometimes easier to cut a stone "out of proportion" than to adhere to the strict guidelines.

[4] *The Diamond Dictionary,* p. 296.

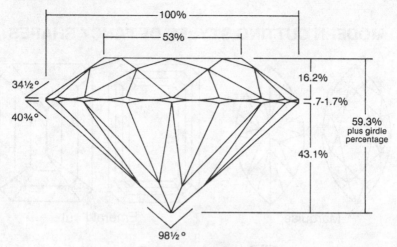

Tolkowsky theoretical brilliant cut
redrawn from *Gaal's Diamond Dictionary*

Not all stones, after all, can be easily cut to the ideal proportions without losing additional weight—and as long as carat weight continues to impress buyers, cutting will suffer by comparison.

I saw a pair of rough stones a couple of years ago whose history illustrates my point. They were of almost an identical weight, varying by only a couple of points, and were about to be cut into either one-carat or 75-point stones. There was plenty of "excess" rough stone to allow for either of these weights, and the only choice to be made was whether to make the stones smaller but more brilliant, or larger and less brilliant.

It was decided to try one of each, and the cutter—an experienced and able artisan—set to work. When he finished, he showed me the two cut specimens. The one which had ended up weighing one carat was of exactly the same color and clarity as the 75-point one, but there was no question which was the superior stone. In "saving on weight" with the larger stone, the cutter had made its pavilion quite a bit deeper than "ideal" and also "spread" the crown out so that it was larger than was really desirable. The result was a so-so diamond. The 75-point diamond, on the other hand, was a superb piece of work. It had been cut extremely close to the "ideal," and it displayed remarkable fire and brilliance.

There was no question in my mind which was the superior gem, and yet I knew that the inferior but larger stone would bring more on the market than the smaller but more exact one. That turned out to be the

MODERN CUTTING STYLES OF FANCY SHAPES

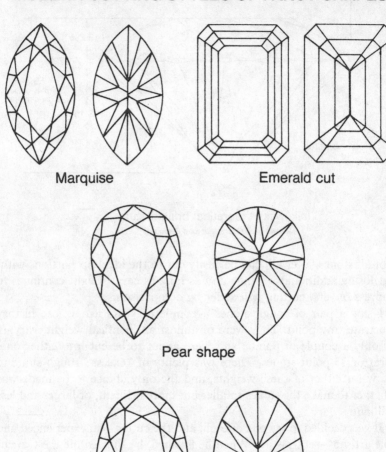

Marquise

Emerald cut

Pear shape

Oval

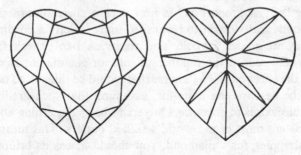

Heart

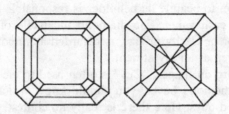

Square emerald cut

Additional crown variations in modern fancy shapes

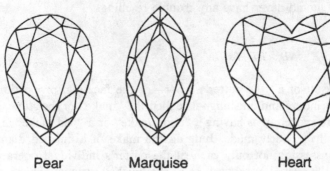

Pear   Marquise   Heart

case. Later in the week I learned that the small gem had been sold for $1,000 and the large one for four times that much. Was it really worth $4,000? That's very doubtful.

Cutting "out of proportion" is now such a common practice that I feel diamonds really ought to be graded more strictly according to cut, just as they are graded for color and clarity. A 1-to-10 scale for proper cutting would reduce the number of inferior-cut diamonds quickly— although the effect on the selling market would be difficult to determine. Perhaps the best we can hope for, assuming that such grading is not soon established, is to encourage buyers to be as discerning about judging cuts as are most of the world's skilled cutters. This means that, if you are shopping for a diamond, you should assess its brilliance with just as much care as you do its color or its clarity. I am in agreement with Marc Hudgeons when he says, "The ability of a diamond to enchant, to dazzle, to beguile its beholder is responsible for a very large measure of its cash value. The diamond incapable of doing this, no matter the color or clarity or size, is regarded as impotent and should not be considered as an investment."[5]

Finally, a word on shapes. "Cut" is often used to mean "shape," and as a potential diamond buyer, you should know which cuts are most likely to be good buys. Here there is really no contest. Although all of the basic cuts have their champions, the round, or brilliant, cut is far and away the most popular cut today. It is always in demand, and for that reason it is still the best buy. The popularity of the other shapes comes and goes, but the brilliant retains its appeal. It is the one shape that you should never have any trouble reselling.

THE MAKE AND THE TAKE

The result of all the cutter's labor—of the faceting, proportioning, sawing, grinding and finishing—is called the "make" of the stone. Diamonds are spoken of as having a "good make" or a "bad make" and of being well or poorly made. Judging the make of a finished diamond involves assessing not only each of the cutter's individual operations, but also the overall attractiveness of the finished product. This kind of judgment, which was fairly rare in the days when size alone was considered crucial to a stone's value, is becoming more common today— although, as I've noted, the prejudice for size still exists. As diamond historian Herbert Tillander has noted, make is now a "quality factor,"

[5] Hudgeons, *Official Investors Guide to Buying and Selling Gold, Silver and Diamonds.*

involving "an intelligent appreciation of the overall beauty of the diamond, without an exaggerated examination of details."[6]

You cannot develop that kind of appreciation overnight, but it is a
worthy goal to aim for. For if a diamond does not enchant you as you
look at it, if it does not impress you with its almost magical light, half of
its value is gone. Unlike gold and silver, diamonds are not tied directly
to currency values: their value is far more a matter of aesthetic appeal.
So even if you are buying them as an investment or a hedge against
inflation, you should be sure that you buy *beautiful* specimens. If they
are not beautiful to you, they are not going to be beautiful, probably, to
the person you want to sell them to years from now.

Assessing a diamond's beauty means paying careful attention to all
the four C's and then weighing them against one another. In some cases
this will mean you have to sacrifice something of color to get a stone of
better clarity. In others it means you will have to settle for a smaller
stone than you had in mind because the cut is so superior. You have to
learn to balance the C's against each other, because, unless you have an
unlimited amount of money to spend or invest, you will never be able to
get all four of the highest quality in the same stone. Naturally the most
desirable buy in diamonds is a large D-flawless stone of perfect proportions, but as I've already mentioned, there are probably no more than a
handful of them on the market at any one time. What you should aim
for is not this unattainable ideal, but smaller, well-made brilliants. Buying one-carat rounds of reasonable color and clarity is still probably
your best way of assuring that your "take," when you go to resell them,
will be high.

But even if you pay strict attention to the four C's, you can still
become part of somebody else's "take" unless you also keep an eye out
for frauds. There are plenty of "cats and dogs" being sold as investment
diamonds these days, and many people have been ruined financially by
leaping on the investment bandwagon before they looked where it was
going. It is to help you avoid joining them that the next chapter is
written.

---

[6] In Legrand, *Diamonds: Myth, Magic, and Reality,* p. 201.

CHAPTER 9

THE SMART DIAMOND SHOPPER

In the middle of the late-1970s recession, a classified advertisement in the New York *Times* promised "experienced telephone pros" an employment opportunity that was billed as "the best job in town." The job, it turned out, was selling "investment quality diamonds," and for many of the people who responded to the ad, the promise proved to be quite honest. A great deal more honest, in any case, than the job that the pros were hired to do.

The people who answered this ad and others like it, and who were eventually hired by investment diamond firms, were not expected to know anything about diamonds. What they were expected to know was how to talk on the telephone: how to make a presentation—for diamonds, for real estate or for doughnuts—sound so attractive that the person on the other end of the line would be unable to resist. These "boiler room" operators, as they were soon dubbed by the press, were remarkably successful in their phone pitches. Working for 5 or 10 percent commissions on the diamonds they sold, some of them were soon making $100,000 a year—which meant that the most successful among them were selling millions of dollars' worth of diamonds a year to their clients.

These clients were not nearly as successful as the salesmen from whom they bought their "investments." Assured by the slick talkers that they were purchasing gems of guaranteed investment quality, many of them found, when they tried to resell the diamonds a couple of years later, that their actual resale value was far less than the price they had paid. Others paid out hard cash for diamonds that never even existed—and got nothing but "paper diamonds" for their pains. Still others didn't even get the paper: they sent their checks off to a post-office-box number somewhere in Arizona, waited three months for their stones and, upon calling up Arizona information to get the investment firm's number, discovered that it had never existed.

In the recession-torn days of the late 1970s, hundreds of people fearful of inflation lost money in phony investment schemes, and several of those schemes involved so-called "investment quality diamonds." To the novice investor today, the sad tale of these phony schemes is an object lesson in how *not* to buy diamonds. Some of the more blatantly dishonest firms have now gone out of business—or been put out of business by the government—but there are plenty of sharp operators still around, and because investment-diamond scams are still going on, I want to start this cautionary chapter by describing how they have worked since the 1970s.

THE INVESTMENT-DIAMOND CRAZE

The most notorious of the phony investment diamond firms of the 1970s was an Arizona outfit that had the gall to call itself De Beers Diamond Investment, Ltd. Although the company had no connection whatsoever with the South African De Beers, potential clients who were ignorant of the diamond world did not realize that—and the Arizona firm took advantage of their ignorance to bilk them out of literally millions of dollars.

The way the phony De Beers—and numerous other investment firms, many of them in Arizona—worked was this. After hiring their "telephone pros," they set up a system of WATS lines and began putting ads in the popular press offering toll-free calls to clients who were interested in a "surefire hedge against inflation." At the same time, they secured lists of people with obvious capital—doctors and dentists were the favorite targets—and began calling them directly, promising the same surefire opportunity. The salesmen painted glowing pictures of the solid history of diamond appreciation and correspondingly grim pictures of what would happen to their clients' nest eggs if they didn't immediately take advantage of the offers.

In some cases, the stones that the Arizona De Beers offered for sale were not even diamonds at all, but low-grade colored stones of almost no value. In other cases, phony investment firms didn't have *anything* to sell and lured customers into sending on their checks by the mere *promise* of riches. In most cases, however, what they sold their clients were real diamonds, but diamonds that were incredibly overpriced and overgraded in terms of the market at the time. Told that he could have a genuine "investment quality" or "excellent quality" diamond for a mere $5,000 a carat, the unsuspecting investor didn't bother to ask what "investment quality" meant—and ended up purchasing a stone that was off color and ill cut for a price that only a fine-cut D flawless should have commanded.

It was the widespread anxiety over inflation that kept these firms in business. People who had salted away several thousand dollars as protection for their future were persuaded in many cases to take that money out of their savings accounts and put it into an investment that was guaranteed to appreciate—as savings accounts were not—far faster than the rate of inflation. The quick-talking salesmen pointed to the fact that diamonds had been appreciating at a steady, healthy rate for many years—and that in the past couple of years they had really begun to skyrocket. There was still time, the naïve physician was told, to lock in his future earnings at a staggering appreciation rate—but only if he acted right now. Many of the "De Beers" marks did act immediately—and lost their entire savings.

Because diamonds have appreciated steadily in value over the years, I feel they are a fairly sound investment: they are a controlled article of proven public appeal; production and marketing are strictly limited; and if you hold on to them long enough (five years would be about the minimum), they are almost certain to increase in value. The trouble with the promises made by the phony investment houses (and even by some houses that were relatively scrupulous in their dealings) was that they pitched their diamonds as if they would guarantee a quick killing *as well as* a long-term hedge.

You cannot have it both ways. Either diamonds are a sound long-range hedge or they have the capability of making you rich overnight. Novice investors in the 1970s and early 1980s tried to have their cake and eat it too—and in the process they lost a great deal. In effect, they paid speculative prices for stones that should have commanded only moderately bullish prices, and when the bottom dropped out of the investment diamond market, they were left with grossly overpriced gems.

The average wholesale price, for example, for the equivalent of a one-carat D-flawless diamond in 1972 was about $2,000. In normal times, that price would have risen at a rate of about 5 to 10 percent a year, so that by the end of the decade the stone would have been worth $3,000 to $4,000. But because of the investment diamond craze of the mid-1970s, that is not what happened. Italian investors reacting to a falling *lira,* Arab investors wanting to stockpile something even more valuable than oil and finally American investors wanting to get on the diamond bandwagon all started to boost the value of the gems, so that they rose much more swiftly than anybody had expected. In spite of the South African De Beers official stand against investment diamonds, the market was out of control, with hundreds of inflation-wary people trying simultaneously to protect their futures and make a quick buck. By 1980 the going rate for that one-carat D-flawless was an astonishing $60,000!

This enormous surge in the price of the best diamonds was, of course, aided by the phony Arizona De Beers and other investment firms. The survival of their lucrative game depended on the price continuing to rise and on people continuing to believe that their investment purchases were all of the same top quality.

That is where some of the deception came in. I said before that there are never more than a handful of D-flawless diamonds on the market at any given time. But to lure investors into buying, the phony firms started selling lower-quality gems for the same prices that the top-quality ones had commanded. The prices of investment diamonds continued to rise well after most of the real investment-quality gems were off the market, so that by the end of the 1970s, investors were paying collectors prices for stones that were only good for jewelry—and for some that were not even that good.

Some observers thought that the trend would continue indefinitely—which is just what the Arizona firms wanted them to think. Even as astute an observer as Marc Hudgeons wrote, in 1981, that by 1983 the price of a D-flawless would be up to $100,000—and that the price of lesser gems would rise accordingly.[1] That is not what happened. Eventually the speculators realized that the price had been overinflated and began to sell off their gems. This unpredicted profit taking, combined with a growing realization that many stones were simply overpriced (that is, were not what their sellers said they were), led to a rapid price fall. By late 1982, the price of that one-carat D-flawless—the one that had been $2,000 in 1972 and $60,000 in 1980—had fallen to the still high but more reasonable level of $20,000.

Of course, if you had bought that stone in 1972 or before, you still would have realized a good profit: $20,000 on a $2,000 stone in ten years is certainly a respectable advance. But if you had purchased the stone in the midst of the investment craze, you would not have made out so well. What happened to diamonds by the end of that craze is exactly what happened to gold and silver in the same time period: the initial rush to purchase a "hot" item had been cooled off by market forces and also by speculators' apprehension that, unless a stop was put to the escalation, the whole bottom would fall out of the market.

Fortunately for the novice investor, the investment diamond craze is now pretty well spent. The Arizona De Beers, which made an estimated $50 million in its heyday, is now under indictment by the federal government, and many of the other big investment firms have also ceased

[1] Hudgeons, op. cit., p. 176.

operation. As a result, this is a much better time to consider purchasing diamonds than the past several years has been.

But this does not mean that all the danger is past. On the contrary. The really big-time boiler-room boys may be out of business, but there are still plenty of tricks to watch out for. Many of the more common ones have to do with just what the phony De Beers specialized in: overgrading and overpricing the stones.

PRICING: HOW MUCH IS IT REALLY WORTH?

Murray Schumach tells an amusing story in his book *The Diamond People* which relates to the complexity and variability of gem pricing. In the spring of 1979, he writes, a dealer bought a diamond for $16,000. In late summer, he sold it for $22,000. A week later it was resold for $29,000, and a few days after that, it changed hands again—this time for $32,000. A pundit, hearing the story of the continuing escalation in price, remarked, "If that stone ever leaves the Street, half a dozen people could go out of business." (The Street, of course, was New York's famous 47th Street.)

This anecdote indicates more than the fact that late 1979 was the height of the investment diamond craze. It shows an aspect of the diamond world that is prevalent even in times of relative economic stability: the fact that prices for diamonds can often change very rapidly as the stones change hands. They may not always go up at the rate indicated in this story, but go up they do, practically every time they are sold. I have seen diamonds change hands three or four times in one day, with the final buyer paying much more than the original asking price.

Obviously this cannot be explained simply by invoking the catchall of inflation. Nothing, not even diamonds, realistically appreciates 50 percent in value between breakfast and dinner—and yet this happens to the price of diamonds all the time. The main reason is that everyone involved in the selling of a stone must make his or her personal profit; the more middlemen involved, the more the price is going to rise. Since the turnaround in diamonds is so rapid, it's understandable that price rises like this are common.

In addition, of course, diamond sellers want to get as much as they can for a given stone, and since there is no central pricing control mechanism on the retail level (like the CSO's mechanism for roughs), there are bound to be numerous cases of diamonds being sold at unreasonably high prices to buyers who are ignorant of their true worth. Not all diamond sales happen between professionals, and the interest of so many amateurs in the stones naturally drives selling prices up.

But it doesn't drive them up uniformly everywhere. The prices of diamonds are not only often unreasonably high; they are also mystifyingly varied. The price of a given stone is really only the price that can be had for it at a given place and at a given time. In a sense, it is misleading to speak of a one-carat D-flawless being "worth" $20,000 today. That is an average figure; the real "worth" of that stone is what Mr. Jackson will give to Mr. Perlman in his shop on 47th Street at 4 P.M. Tuesday afternoon, or—if Mr. Jackson decides not to buy it—what Mrs. Green will give for it fifteen minutes later.

To you, the novice diamond shopper, this means that a cardinal rule of thumb in diamond buying—as in buying precious metals—is that you should always *shop around* before you make a purchase. This is actually much more important in diamonds than it is in either silver or gold, because while the commissions and fees on precious metals are fairly uniform (although far from constant), dealers' fees on diamonds vary tremendously. And it is dealers' fees—and the fees of other middlemen—that eventually drive the prices of diamonds up. It's the various sellers' profit margins plus the market value that you are really paying for when you purchase a stone.

There's nothing wrong with this. If it weren't for the middlemen, that spotless E-flawless you've been admiring would still be a hunk of oily rough in Zaire. You should expect to pay dealers' fees—that's what keeps diamonds a thriving business. But you should not expect to pay more in markup costs than the diamond itself is worth. Most reputable dealers work on approximately a 10 to 30 percent markup. That is, for a stone that they buy wholesale at $10,000, you should expect to pay no more than about $13,000 retail. This is an acceptable level of profit in the business; just watch out for dealers who charge much higher rates. Most investment diamond firms, for example, work at about a 25 percent commission, and in the heyday of the investment craze many were pulling in 50 to 100 percent markups.

Moreover, the same firms that commonly charge a 25 percent markup over wholesale make an additional profit when *buying* stones, since they pay considerably less—sometimes as much as 20 percent less —than the average resale price when you go to resell your goods. Say a firm like this gets a small G stone of reasonable clarity and pays $1,000 for it wholesale. It will sell that stone to you for $1,250, and buy it back from you for only $800. That's $450 differential on a stone that cost them only $1,000 in the first place.

Buying a stone at a fair price is further complicated by the fact that many good stones are overgraded when they are sold to the public and undergraded when they are bought back. This is especially true with the better-color (D to G) stones and is so common in the industry that it has come to be considered accepted practice. Variable grading goes on at every level of diamond dealing, too. When your local diamond dealer purchases an "iffy" stone wholesale, he will naturally try to get it at the lowest price he can—and often this means that he will grade it himself one color lower than he believes it to be. If it looks like an F stone to him under his loupe, he'll tell the seller it's a G. The seller will tell him, of course, that it's an E—and unless the stone has a certificate specifying its color (more about certificates in a minute), they will have to bargain until they agree on the stone's "real" color. As a retail buyer, you don't have the advantage, usually, of being able to bargain like this: you are simply told by the seller that such-and-such a stone is an "excellent" E-color stone—even though he may have paid only an F- or a G-color price for it.

Many people attempt to get around the hazards of overgrading and subsequent overpricing by having their potential purchases independently appraised. This is generally a wise approach, but there are problems inherent in it too. Most appraisers work on a 1 percent commission basis: the fee they charge you for appraising your stone is based on 1 percent of the value of the stone. This leads to an obvious problem. If the appraiser knows that he is going to get 1 percent from you no matter how much the stone is worth, it's obviously to his advantage to appraise it as high as he can, since that will make him more money. It's extremely common, therefore, for stones to be appraised too highly and for all but the most scrupulous appraisers to call your G stone an F and your VVS_2 a VVS_1. This may give you a momentary thrill, but the thrill will disappear when you try to resell the stone and discover it has been graded too high.

Honest confusion also often plays a part. As I've already noted, the determination of color and clarity always involves some subjectivity, and this means that even between perfectly scrupulous people, there is going to be difference of opinion about grading. A big enough difference of opinion can mean a major difference in price.

Unfortunately, there is no control over this somewhat messy situation on the part of "official" bodies. There is no fixed daily price for diamonds as there is for gold and silver, and while the Securities and Exchange Commission and the Federal Trade Commission do regulate cases of actual fraud (or try to), they don't have anything to say about pricing per se. Since there is nothing *illegal* about asking $10,000 for a stone that was bought wholesale for half that much, overpricing goes on all the time. That is why shopping around is crucial. The only thing that really regulates diamond prices on the retail level is competition; the wise shopper takes advantage of that fact to seek out the best available bargains.

But I use that word "bargain" with caution. You should always keep in mind, when you are shopping for diamonds, that while overpricing is a common hazard, underpricing can be just as much trouble. That is because there is no such thing as real "underpricing." The incredible bargain you are being offered on that stunning D-flawless stone may turn out to be no bargain at all, because it is not a D-flawless stone. By all means, be wary of high prices, but be just as wary of very low ones. If you ask five dealers to show you a one-carat G-color stone, you will probably get five different prices. If one of those prices is half the amount of the others, there is a very good chance that the dealer with the irresistible bargain is not such a fool as he looks: unless you want to play the fool yourself, you should look for your "bargains" within a reasonable range of deviation from the industry "norm" at any given time. A 15 percent "savings" on a stone might reasonably make you eager; a 50 percent "savings" should only make you suspicious.

TRICKS OF THE TRADE

Overpricing is not in itself illegal, and although it is pretty common in the diamond business, it's by no means the only hazard that you have to watch out for. Diamond selling also involves numerous clearly illegal practices—practices that, if they are discovered (which is never easy), will lead to SEC or FTC investigation and prosecution.

1. Misrepresentation

This is probably the most common of all unscrupulous dealers' tricks. Misrepresentation can refer to many things. A dealer might misrepresent the carat weight of a stone by using dishonest scales. He might misrepresent the color of a stone by using an inaccurate master set, or simply by relying on the potential buyer's ignorance of color. He might misrepresent a stone's clarity by failing to point out a flaw; some shady operators even offer to let their customers inspect imperfect stones themselves under a ten-power lens, knowing very well that they wouldn't know a pinpoint from a feather if they looked through the loupe all day. Or they might misrepresent the fire and brilliance of an inferior cut by showing the customer a stone under unduly strong lighting designed to enhance the play of lights. In all these cases, the dishonest dealer is clearly relying on his own superior knowledge about the gems to convince a relatively naïve person that they are something they are not. That is why the more you know about the four C's before you walk into a shop—the more homework you have done—the less likely you are to be taken.

2. Repolishing

I mentioned in the last chapter that diamonds with surface blemishes are often "recut" or "repolished" in order to remove these imperfections. When this is done well, it does not harm the stone, although it does reduce its carat weight. In some cases, however, this recutting is done for ulterior motives, and in many of these cases the real value of the stones is sharply reduced—although the purchaser may not know it.

Repolishing can destroy the "make" of a stone if it is done improperly, and this is not an uncommon practice among dealers who care more about size and color than shape. Ideally when a stone is recut, all its facets—this usually means fifty-eight facets—must be repolished equally, so the overall symmetry is maintained. But this is not always done. Often only a few facets are repolished, thus removing the unwanted blemish but sacrificing symmetry. This is done particularly when the blemish is on the table of the stone, and this can severely impair the stone's appearance—although the destruction may be invisible to the novice diamond buyer.

In addition, repolishing is often done on stolen stones to conceal their true identity. No two cut diamonds are exactly alike in make, and due to their uniqueness, high-quality stones are often "fingerprinted" by a laser identification process, and their unique identities are then fed into a computer. Referring to these "gem print" records, a person can tell his or her diamond from any other one on earth. To get around this identification process, diamond thieves often pay a modest recutting fee (it's usually around $75 to $150 per carat), utterly changing the stolen gem's unique nature.

Say a thief had a 420-point diamond, that is, a 4.20-carat gem. If he wanted to disguise it from the police, he could arrange to have it repolished slightly so it would not register in the computer. The cutter might shave just a hair off the table, making the gem a 4.17-carat diamond. This slight difference in weight would have only a small effect on the price, but it would completely change the diamond's identity. If the thief were apprehended and the diamond confiscated, the original owner would have an extremely difficult time proving that the stolen gem was his, because there would be no computer record of such a 4.17-carat diamond.

Even when it is not used illegally like this, repolishing is sometimes of dubious ethical value because it permits a dealer to impair a stone's original beauty while adding to its selling price. This type of cutting is sometimes done to keep a diamond at a full carat when proper cutting would reduce its size to .85 or .95 carat. Especially if the color is poor or the diamond is quite imperfect, it pays the cutter to keep a one-carat weight of improper proportions, rather than cut a better but smaller diamond. Only if the diamond is of very good color and the clarity can be improved by cutting does it pay to cut out an imperfection and get a finer-quality, smaller stone.

Suppose, for example, that a given stone weighs 1.03 carats and the grade is H/VS$_2$. If the cutter recuts to remove a feather on this stone, he can achieve a grade of H/VS$_1$, but he will end up with a .95-carat stone. If, on the other hand, he finishes it at one carat, the stone may bring a better price, even though the sacrifice on the make has significantly reduced its true value. It would be an illusion in this case to suppose that the greater weight means higher value but many buyers, oblivious to "make," labor under just this illusion.

3. Coloring

Another unethical way of increasing the value of a diamond is to change its original color by various painting, or "coating," processes. Diamonds have been altered in this way for years, but recent technological developments have made coloring a more serious problem than it used to be, because "coated" stones are less easy to detect. The most common old-fashioned way of "coloring" a stone was to paint it with a mixture of indelible ink and alcohol. This was actually a type of "decoloring," since it disguised the natural yellow of inferior stones and allowed them to be graded up one or two levels: naturally, this could significantly increase the price.

Fortunately this old coating process was fairly easy to discern. Exposing the coated diamond to steam or more alcohol generally washed the covering off. A recent process, however, makes discovery much more difficult, because the coating developed by "diamond artists," as they are called, cannot be readily detected: it is "baked on" the stone. This poses problems for the appraiser, and of course for the diamond buyer.

Coloring is also done to *impart* color to a stone, rather than remove it. You will remember that "fancy" diamonds—diamonds with a distinct pink or yellow or blue color—often command better prices than the finest colorless grades. Because this is so, off-white diamonds have long been artificially colored by a variety of technological processes. The most common process is radiation, in which the stone is exposed to radioactivity, which alters its chemical structure. Because of radiation (and to a lesser extent, lasers), many of today's fancy diamonds were made, not born, that way.

Coloring diamonds in this manner is neither illegal nor unethical—as long as the buyer is aware that what he is getting is an artificially enhanced gem. Unlike the coating processes, radiation *permanently* alters the stone's color, and this means that the resulting diamond is not so much a disguised gem as a thoroughly remade one. Irradiated diamonds are not as valuable as naturally fancy diamonds, and there definitely is fraud involved in cases where a seller tries to pass off an artificially colored stone as a natural. But as long as the coloring is not concealed, selling irradiated gems is a perfectly acceptable practice.

Some people even ask to have their diamonds colored, preferring fancies to "plain" diamonds. This may enhance the value and the beauty—as long as you didn't start with a colorless stone. Having an off-white stone coated is not at all uncommon among people who want to improve the appearance of their gems. Again, there is nothing the matter with this, as long as you don't subsequently try to sell the altered stone as a natural. Generally it doesn't enhance the value; it just fools your friends.

4. Fakes

Finally, a word should be said about diamonds that are not really diamonds. I will mention imitation and synthetic diamonds in the following chapter, since strictly speaking they are moderately priced stones, rather than diamonds. But I do want to make you aware here that the selling of "paste" and "glass" and other nondiamond "gems" has by no means come to an end. When this is done aboveboard, there is nothing wrong with it: if you like the look of cubic zirconia, by all means buy it in favor of diamonds. But do not delude yourself into thinking that you are purchasing an investment. No fake diamond is an investment, so if you are shopping for stones for their investment value, you should steer away from cubics entirely. Again, you might fool your friends, but you will not fool a dealer if you try to sell.

Because only an expert can readily tell a fake diamond from a real one, you should always avoid shops whose reputation you cannot easily verify. Passing off glass as the real stuff is still something that happens every day. Know your seller. It's the only way of avoiding getting stuck with a worthless "gem."

Beware particularly of diamonds with unusual or unfamiliar names. Many of these are not diamonds at all. "Pennsylvania diamond," for example, is a common misnomer for pyrite, while rock crystal, one of the most common diamond substitutes in cheap jewelry, goes under the equally erroneous names of Herkimer diamond, Bristol diamond, Trenton diamond and Pecos diamond. The names refer to the sites where these crystals originate: they do not specify "rare" or "unusual" types of diamond.

PROTECTING YOURSELF

All of what I've said here, I hope, has made it clear to you that Rule #1 of diamond shopping is to know whom you're dealing with. Shopping around is essential not only to compare prices, but also to compare reputations. All that I said in previous chapters about checking into the background of your seller applies here, too. It is a major purpose of the Better Business Bureau to serve as a watchdog for the public: ask their advice if you have any doubt about the reputability of a diamond firm. Call the attorney general in your state. Check with the SEC and the FTC to see if Friendly Fred is currently under investigation. And in general steer away from places that have been in business only a short time. Stick with the established firms.

Find out specifically what your firm's buy-back policy is on its diamonds. No firm can, legally or practically, guarantee you that it will buy back your gems at a profit to you, and you should be wary of any firm that makes this claim. But you should also be assured that, if for any reason you are dissatisfied with your gems when you get them home, the firm will repurchase them at no loss to you. Get a written guarantee that the dealer will take the stone back, with no loss, within a specified amount of time: two or three weeks of grace time will give you a chance to have the stone appraised elsewhere, and you can then decide whether or not it's worth holding on to. If the dealer will not guarantee such a buy-back, take your business elsewhere.

One of the most insidious practices of the late 1970s investment firms was what Murray Schumach calls the "Catch-22 of the diamond investment scam." He quotes a diamond merchant describing how this practice worked:

> You buy a diamond. You are told the weight. It comes in a plastic container. If you take it to an appraiser to judge the color or clarity, he can't do this properly unless he removes the stone from the container. But if he does this, then the company that sold you the diamond says it is not obligated to take it back.[2]

[2] *The Diamond People*, pp. 199–200.

This type of chicanery is still going on. It is simply a way for a dishonest dealer to avoid having someone else check up on the validity of his claims. You should bypass entirely any seller who is afraid to have you look at his goods without the specious protection of a plastic container. All he is trying to do is sidestep the buy-back guarantee.

I realize that advising you to deal only with old, reliable firms is rather vague advice. Checking with the Better Business Bureau and the government agencies covering fraud is a start in weeding out the bad dealers, but where do you go from there? Is there any further assurance for the novice diamond investor who wants to avoid being cheated?

There is no surefire guarantee, but there are a couple of things you can watch for to make your shopping around easier. One is a sticker on the dealer's window indicating that he or she is a member of the American Gem Society. This society was established in 1934 as a kind of internal regulatory commission. According to the society's descriptive brochure on diamonds, it is composed of jewelers "pledged to the vigilant protection of the buying public, and to the maintenance of fine business standards and practices of its members." Since the society is somewhat selective, buying from one of its members gives you fairly good assurance that you will not be cheated, or at least not be subjected to devious practices. You may still end up paying a stiff price for your diamond, but that is not illegal.

The other thing you can watch for—indeed, insist upon—is a certificate from the GIA. The Gemological Institute of America, which maintains offices in New York and Los Angeles, was established in 1931 to bring some order into the then perplexing world of diamond grading, by educating gemologists in evaluating gemstones and ultimately by setting up its own classification system. Although many organizations continue to grade diamonds, the certificates issued by the GIA are today considered the most reliable and impartial guides to the four C's of these stones. Any diamonds you buy for investment purposes should be accompanied by a GIA certificate. In the confusing world of diamond selling, this certificate is the best evidence you can get that you are buying what you think you are buying.

The GIA does not actually value diamonds for you, but it does give you an exact and consistent guide to the elements that appraisers take into account. The GIA certificate identifies how your diamond stacks up to diamonds in general in terms of the four C's. The shape and cut—height and measurements—of the diamond are listed, as are its proportions. The finish of the diamond is rated in terms of its polish and symmetry. The stone is also graded according to clarity and color. Any internal or external characteristics of the stone are also pinpointed on two accompanying diagrams. This certificate is a unique "identity card" for your stone, one that enables anyone interested to tell your stone apart from any that may resemble it. In fact, the GIA can now even inscribe a certification number on the girdle of a diamond by laser, without changing the quality of the stone.

Even with its certificates and its lasers, the GIA has not entirely eliminated fraud and confusion. But in a field from which it is impossible to eliminate subjectivity and chicanery altogether, the GIA has done pretty well. Its certificates are universally respected among dealers and are considered so reliable that sometimes diamonds are sold "long distance" on the basis of these certificates alone. If Mr. Johnson in Sioux City, Iowa, wants to "inspect" a stone from New York, he may ask simply to see the stone's certificate, and make the purchase without first seeing the diamond.

When you are shopping for investment diamonds, you must insist on GIA certification: if a dealer dismisses this as unimportant, dismiss him —he does not know, or does not want you to know, investment-quality diamonds. Furthermore, if a stone in which you are interested was certified several years ago, before the investment craze, you may want to have it recertified before you purchase it. Grading was thrown into a turmoil by the investment surge, and as a result, older stones sometimes do not mesh, in terms of similarity of grading, with the newer ones. You will have to pay for such a recertification yourself, but in most cases it will be worth the fee. Your jeweler will have to send the stone to the GIA for you, under a new policy, and you will pay a recertification fee ranging from about $25 for a half-carat diamond up to $500 for one of twenty to twenty-five carats. If you buy a stone on the basis of an old certificate, you may find when you get the diamond home that it has acquired a scratch in the meantime, or even that an internal flaw which was not noticed ten years ago is now visible, because of improved GIA technology. This could mean that the stone is less valuable than the old certificate indicates.

Ten years ago, almost no stones were certified. Today, due to improved technology and heightened awareness on the part of investors, virtually all good stones are certified and most carry GIA certificates. The certificates of other grading organizations, such as the European Gemological Institute, tend to be a little less widely recognized than the GIA's. You should avoid entirely any dealer who assures you that, according to his own grading system, a given stone is "excellent" or "top grade." Such personal grading systems are meaningless, even when they are not actually deceptive.

Certification is often referred to in the industry as the "fifth C." That will give you an idea of how highly the GIA is regarded. The presence of a GIA certificate does not mean that you will always get a great buy. But buying diamonds that don't have one is like shooting at a target blindfolded. The GIA certificate remains the smart diamond shopper's best single means of protection.

PART **IV**

JEWELS AND JEWELRY

CHAPTER 10

WHEN IS A RUBY NOT A RUBY?

Investing in gold, silver and diamonds has traditionally been a prerogative of the relatively well-to-do. Scared off by the supposed high sums needed to enter the precious-metals and diamond markets, many would-be investors have preferred to stick with "safer" commodities like soybeans or timber stocks, leaving the "glamour" commodities to speculators who could afford heavy losses.

As we've seen in the preceding chapters, this situation has been changing in recent years, as inflation and fears of domestic crises have forced formerly timid investors to put their trust, however nervously, into assets that are less mercurial than money. Due to the international monetary troubles of the 1970s, investment in gold, silver and diamonds has widened considerably, and people who a decade ago would not have thought about buying a Krugerrand are now purchasing them in large quantities. You no longer have to be a prince—even a merchant prince—to own precious metals, and indeed one of the principal aims of this book has been to show you how you can, with a minimum of risk, buy and sell the glamour commodities no matter what your income.

But traditions die hard, and in spite of the investment revolutions of the inflationary 1970s, many people with only a little money to invest still think along traditional lines. They do not think in terms of fine gold or pre-1965 quarters or D-flawless stones, but in terms of the more conventional "investment" of jewelry. Because jewelry has traditionally been associated with great wealth, and because diamond rings and gold chains are now priced within nearly everyone's reach, it is commonly assumed that if you have a few hundred dollars to invest, buying a good brooch or bracelet is a sound way of putting your money into something that not only is beautiful to behold but will appreciate steadily in value over the years.

Because jewelry is still such a popular "investment" vehicle, I want to devote the final section of this book to demonstrating that, even though the component parts of a diamond ring may be fairly safe buys, purchasing the ring itself—as an investment—is almost never a good idea. Jewelry is, to be sure, an attractive and generally durable way of translating your savings into something "harder" than money. But, for a number of reasons, considering jewelry as an investment is, with very few exceptions, a serious error of judgment. In this chapter and the next, I will show you why this is so—and explain why, if you have only that few hundred dollars to spend, you are much better advised to put it into the pure, unadorned metal or stone than into the composite bracelet or ring.

There are two principal reasons why buying jewelry, although it may be very gratifying to the eye and the ego, is not a good investment policy. The first reason—the prevalence of imitation and fraud in the jewelry market—I will discuss in this chapter. The second—the markup system, which prohibitively escalates retail prices—I will go into in the next.

LESS THAN MEETS THE EYE

In eighteenth-century England, as urbanism and industrialism created a rising middle class with increasingly expensive tastes, a social need arose for jewelry that was as attractive as that worn by the aristocracy but that could be purchased at less exorbitant prices than the aristocracy were accustomed to paying. The new middle class felt they deserved the adornments of the very rich but were not prepared to pay the going rate for them—and so, as a kind of consolation, they called for reasonable imitations—ones that the new money could afford.

The call was answered by a host of entrepreneurial inventors, the chief of whom were the London clockmaker Christopher Pinchbeck and a young physician's assistant by the name of James Tassie. Around the beginning of the eighteenth century, Pinchbeck devised an alloy of copper and zinc which, to the uneducated eye, bore a pretty fair resemblance to gold. Tassie developed a glassy paste which, after it was shaped and colored, would harden into a remarkably close imitation of diamonds and other precious gems. So popular were these two men's creations that, even today, "pinchbeck" is used to refer to many cheap imitations of gold, while "paste" remains among the most common terms for glass imitations of diamonds.

There were other imitations too, of course. I have already mentioned that "German silver" is still commonly passed off as real silver; that "sterling" is often stamped on silver with less than the requisite .925 fineness; that "solid gold" items often turn out to be merely gold-plated or 8-karat gold, and that several of the popular breeds of "diamonds"—such as "Bristol" and "Pecos"—are not diamonds at all, but rock crystal. The use of substitutes and fakes in the precious-metals and diamond trades is a very old practice and one that has in no way diminished over the years: in fact, thanks to modern technologies (as we saw in the case of "tinted" diamonds), imitation is even more common today than it was years ago—and is even more difficult to detect.

This is especially the case in the jewelry market, and for a good reason. Most of the people who set out to buy pure gold or "investment quality" diamonds have at least a rudimentary notion of what they are looking for. They may still get burned, of course, but they know at least that what they *want* is a certain amount of gold of a certain fineness at a price reasonably close to the spot price. Not even this rudimentary awareness can be assumed for the average purchaser of jewelry. Many of the people who go into a jewelry store to buy a ring are love-struck young couples who don't know—and have no interest in finding out—the difference between a carat and a carrot. Others are big spenders whose idea of a sound purchase is walking away from the store with a rock the size of the Ritz, no matter what the price. Still others are intimidated by the mystique of fine jewelry stores and are thus easy marks for the unscrupulous, who are willing to sell them a "bargain" for only ten times its actual worth.

The average purchaser of jewelry, in short, is a babe in a very thorny wood: goggle-eyed, innocent and prone to disaster at every turn. If he is lucky enough to choose a dealer with high standards of integrity, he may end up with a reasonable buy. But if he is not so lucky, he may end up paying a diamond price for paste, or a bullion price for worthless pinchbeck.

Let's take a hypothetical case. Say that Johnny and Myra Jones are just about to celebrate their tenth wedding anniversary, and Johnny has saved up a thousand dollars to buy Myra a present. He reads that diamonds and gold are always a good investment, and so he determines to put his nest egg down in something that will provide a hedge against inflation as well as bring a sparkle to his wife's eye. Armed with little more than eagerness and affection, he takes his thousand dollars down to a store that has just opened in a shopping center to buy and sell gold, silver and diamonds.

Let's consider this a worse-case scenario and assume that the dealer is not totally honest (which, considering the current jewelry market, is not an outlandish assumption). He shows Johnny a variety of quite tiny diamonds in the thousand-dollar price range, but Johnny finds them a bit small for such a grand occasion. "Don't you have something a little larger?" he asks. The dealer is happy to comply. From a drawer underneath the counter he takes out a gold-and-diamond bracelet which he is sure will take the young man's fancy.

He's right. It's a simple, elegant gold band studded with three fairly large diamonds set a half inch apart in the gold. To Johnny's untrained eye, they sparkle like the Koh-i-noor itself, and—wonder of wonders— the price of the remarkable bracelet is just $999, plus tax. "It's a steal, I'll tell you," says the helpful dealer. "Those are three half-carat stones, and they're good investment quality. You can't go wrong with this one."

Johnny is delighted to have found the bargain, and when he brings the bracelet home, so is Myra. They congratulate each other, drink a little champagne, and close the day confident that, in the years to come, the gift will escalate in value. "It's an insurance policy for the future," Myra says, aware that if they should ever need quick income in their old age, the bracelet will bring many times its current price.

But the story does not end happily. Several years later, an occasion arises when they need some ready cash. Reluctantly they bring the bracelet in to be appraised, consoling themselves for the loss of the memento by acknowledging that this "insurance" aspect of the stones was half the reason for Johnny's purchasing them in the first place. But the appraiser's news is bad. The three stones are half-carat items, all right, but they are not made out of diamond. Rather, they are a combination of earth, alkali and strontium titanate—a common mixture in many of today's best diamond substitutes and one of the many successors to Tassie's original paste.

"What's the bracelet worth, then?" the Joneses ask in dismay.

"Well," the appraiser replies, "the gold is 14-karat, so you might get a hundred dollars for it if you sold it for melting down. The stones go wholesale for about five or ten dollars a carat. I'd say the best you could hope to get for them would be about five dollars."

If the stones had been genuine, he tells them, the bracelet might easily have brought twelve or fifteen hundred dollars on the current market. As it is, they should count themselves lucky if they get a tenth of that in resale.

As I've said, this is a worst-case scenario, but it's important to re- member that it didn't get to be a worst-case scenario just because Johnny was unlucky enough to walk into a dishonest dealer's shop. He contributed to his own fleecing by failing to observe any of the shopping rules that I've been emphasizing throughout this book. Just look at all the things he did wrong:

■ He didn't check on the dealer's reputation before he went shopping, but simply assumed that the guy who had "just opened shop" was all right.

■ He let the dealer know in advance how much he wanted to spend, and asked for the biggest stones he could get for the price.

■ He did not ask to see a GIA certificate or obtain an impartial assessment of the stones—such as an independent appraisal before buying.

■ He was not alert to the fact that, in the world of gold and diamonds, there is very seldom a true "bargain" that is not a fraud in disguise.

Considering all these omissions, Johnny got exactly what should have been expected in the situation. He went out hunting for the "extraordinary," "lucky" buy—and ended up with a lot less than met his eye.

You might think that this kind of chicanery is confined to those aspects of the jewelry trade that can bring in the highest rate of profit: in other words, to the high-draw items such as diamonds and gold. You might think that, because they cost so much less money than diamonds, nobody would bother to fake gems like rubies and pearls. This is not true. If buying jewelry is often considered the poor person's way of investing in precious stones, then buying the lesser precious stones is sometimes seen as the poorer person's way of buying gems. In spite of the diamond explosion of recent years, many people still feel they cannot afford a diamond, and go shopping instead for the "cheaper," colored stones.

This has not had the effect of reducing the prices for these stones, or of eliminating from the trade imitations of every kind of precious stone imaginable. On the contrary, precisely because so many people shop for pearls and emeralds, rather than diamonds, fakery is endemic in the field: each potential mark may not have as much money to lose as the average diamond buyer, but there are so many of them around that it is more than worth the ruby fakers' while to keep coming out with glittering substitutes.

In addition, there are few controls at work in the colored-stones market; this increases the attractiveness of fraud. Even though they don't always work, the GIA and other industry regulations do put a damper on the more obvious diamond fakes. No such regulations exist for colored stones. The GIA will advise you about whether or not a stone is natural, but not about color quality or country of origin. Since geographic origin is so important in determining the value of many colored stones, this means you can easily pay a premium price for a stone that, although it is "genuine," is still worth a fraction of what it would be worth if it came from somewhere else. Run-of-the-mill Thai rubies, for example, are commonly passed off as the much more highly desired Burmese variety. In many cases, dishonest jewelers don't even have to sell you a fake to make an unfair profit; they can simply collect a premium price for a genuine but inferior gem.

A RAINBOW OF RUSES

According to gemologist Eduard Gübelin, gemstones today "constitute the greatest investment in the smallest space."[1] That is true enough in the abstract: what other commodity could give you the equivalent of several thousand dollars in the palm of your hand? But investing in colored stones, like investing in diamonds, can be a very tricky and hazardous business, if you are inattentive to the deceptions that gemstone trading involves.

Colored stones are not really good investments for the novice, because there are no generally accepted standards of judgment in the field and because these stones can so easily be imitated. Particularly because of the popularity of giving "birthstones" as presents, imitations and substitutions have become ubiquitous in the gem industry: there are, after all, only a limited number of fine emeralds available on the market at a given time, so that if a jeweler needs to fill an order for twenty-five emerald birthstones at the end of the month of May, it is almost inevitable that he will supplement his meager stock of fine emeralds with low-quality or even imitation emeralds. Whether or not the customer knows this depends, often enough, not so much on the customer's own eye as on the integrity of the dealer.

The four main categories of gem fakery are the assembling of compound stones, the chemical or radiation treatment of stones, the substitution of gemlike substances for the actual gems and the passing off of poor-quality gems as top-grade specimens.

1. Assembled Stones

As the name implies, an assembled stone is a stone composed of two or more parts put together so that the result resembles a genuine, one-piece stone. GIA director Richard Liddicoat, who coined the term "assembled stone," identifies three major varieties of such composites.[2] A

---

[1] Gübelin, *The Color Treasury of Gemstones,* p. 2.
[2] Liddicoat, *Handbook of Gem Identification,* Ch. XI.

doublet is a stone composed of two parts joined together either by fusion or by a colorless cement. A *triplet* is composed of two parts joined together by a cement that imparts a new color to the joined stone. And a *foilback* is a stone to the back of which a mirrorlike film is adhered, to enhance color or in some cases to suggest a "starlike" appearance.

Doublets, triplets and foilbacks are not illegal, as long as the customer knows what he or she is getting. They become a problem when they are used to disguise the natural color of a stone or to delude the buyer into thinking that he is buying a precious item when in fact he is only getting colored glass.

Liddicoat notes that the four most common examples of assembled stones are the opal doublet, the emerald triplet, the garnet-and-glass doublet and mirror-backed quartz. In the opal doublet, a thin slice of precious opal is glued to a bottom of quartz—thus creating a heavier and more "valuable" stone by adding technically worthless weight. In the emerald triplet, two pieces of inexpensive beryl are joined together by a girdle of green cement, which enhances the color and suggests the stone is an emerald. In the garnet-and-glass doublet, a garnet top is glued to a glass bottom, the composite stone having the dual advantage of rich color, from the glass, and table hardness, from the garnet (see below). In the mirror-backed quartz, a piece of quartz is joined to a blue mirror with a coated back to simulate the internal "star" of a star sapphire.

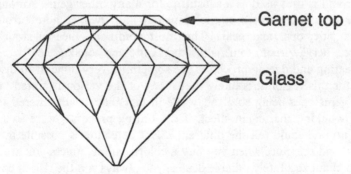

Generally, assembled stones can be detected by microscopic examination. This is easy in the case of foilbacks, since the foil is hard to conceal. Even so, many unwary shoppers are taken in every day by dealers who assure them they have a genuine star sapphire when in fact they have a synthetic. (Technically, a synthetic stone has the same hardness and all the general properties of a real stone. Any other rock is called an imitation.) Unless you are in the habit of carrying a microscope with you everywhere you go, and unless you have a trained eye, this only reinforces what I have said many times before in this book: your best protection against chicanery is to deal only with jewelers of long-standing reputation.

2. Treated Stones

The second category of faked stones is that of stones that have been altered from their natural state by some industrial process. The most common processes are dyeing, heating and irradiation. I have mentioned this already in regard to diamonds and noted that an irradiated diamond, for example, while it may be very beautiful to look at, is never worth as much—to a reputable dealer—as one whose color is the same but natural. Essentially the same thing goes for colored stones. The closer to its pure state a stone is found in, the more valuable it will be. This means that while industrial treatment may enhance the beauty of a given emerald or ruby, it will not—except among the devious—increase its market value.

For most of the common gemstones aside from diamonds, heating and dyeing are more generally used to enhance color than is irradiation. Cornelius Hurlbut and George Switzer note in their text *Gemology*[3] that dyeing is most commonly used on stones that are relatively porous: nonporous stones do not permit adequate penetration of the pigmenting chemicals. Chalcedony, a very porous material, can be dyed almost any color and is thus used as a substitute for many other gems. Among the other commonly tinted stones, Hurlbut and Switzer note turquoise, coral, jade, opal and pearl. The most commonly heated stones are quartz, beryl, zircon, tourmaline, tanzanite and topaz.

Heating and dyeing processes are sometimes very difficult to discern, and for this reason it is likely that many of the variously tinted "natural" gemstones being sold today are in fact industrially altered items. This wouldn't matter, in effect, if the tinting processes were so secure that no one could tell the difference. But detection is possible in most cases, and therefore when you buy a colored stone, unless you are dealing with an absolutely reliable dealer, you always run the risk of coming out with something that, years later, some expert will identify as "treated."

3. Substitutions

Probably the most common means of defrauding the public in the gemstone market is the substitution of base substances for precious

---

[3] Hurlbut and Switzer, *Gemology*, p. 107.

stones, either in a jewelry setting or in their loose, unset states. Tassie has had a long and successful progeny since he made the first widely successful fake diamonds and other gems. Today nearly every valuable gemstone has its imitators—and this situation is likely to continue as long as technology keeps on coming up with ways to copy the minerals.

The most common substitute is still glass in a wide range of hues. Glass is often easy for the expert to spot, due to its relative softness and poor refractive qualities, but this is little help to the novice. The same must be said about the increasingly common use of plastics, especially as substitutes for the opaque gemstones such as amber, lapis lazuli and turquoise. The watchword therefore is caution.

4. Overvaluing

Even when the colored stone you buy is genuine, you can still pay an inflated price if the dealer disguises the poor quality of the stone by emphasizing its "authenticity." I've mentioned that, because stones vary considerably in value depending on geographical origin and other factors, an unscrupulous dealer doesn't have to sell you glass in order to make an unseemly profit. He can sell you a cheap but "real" gem at a top-grade gem's going price and be perfectly within his legal rights. No ethical dealer will sell you an African emerald, for example, at a price that only the best Colombian emeralds should command; unethical jewelers do this all the time. Again, the watchword is caution. Above all, know your dealer. It is notoriously easy for the novice to be deluded by guarantees of "authenticity" in the colored-stone market, and for that reason I advise you never to assume that "genuine" means the same thing as "valuable."

GEMSTONES AND SHAM STONES: A WORKING LIST

Some years ago a customer brought me a deep red stone that he was convinced was a "perfect ruby." How much would I give him for it? he wanted to know. I examined it under my loupe and discovered that it was indeed, as he claimed, a perfect stone. But what this meant, unfortunately for the customer, was that it was obviously *not* a ruby.

True rubies, I explained to him, almost always have minor internal inclusions, formed (as the imperfections of diamonds are formed) at the time of crystallization. The fact that this specimen had no such inclusions was an indication that it was almost certainly not genuine. It was a synthetic, or manufactured, ruby, composed of the same chemical substance as a natural ruby but created artificially in a laboratory. A natural stone of this size and color, I told him, would be worth perhaps $5,000. Precisely because this one was "perfect," it would sell for about $5.00.

The story illustrates a major point to keep in mind when you are considering buying colored stones. Anyone who claims he has a perfect sapphire or a perfect emerald for sale is almost surely trying to unload an imitation. Ironically, it is the small internal disturbances within these precious stones that signify their natural origin and thus vindicate their high selling prices.

But that is only a general caveat to remember when examining gems. To give you more detailed information on specific potential "bargains," let's take a handful of today's more popular gemstones and see how each one can turn out to be something other than what it is supposed to be. The following stones may be considered the Top Ten of the jewelry trade, and as you will see, each one can involve trouble.

1. Diamond

Since I have already devoted three chapters to diamonds, I won't elaborate here on the many cautions you should observe when in the market for these gems. Obviously they are the top of the gemstone line, and because of that they are widely imitated, both honestly and dishonestly. I've already noted that, even when you are looking at genuine natural diamonds, the opportunity for error is very great. It becomes even greater when you are looking not at diamond but glass or one of this stone's other common substitutes.

These include zircon (a natural stone), synthetic sapphire, synthetic spinel, strontium titanate, garnet, Tassie's old standby glass, and cubic zirconia. Cubic zirconia, a synthetic, is by far the most commonly used. Diamonds are also manufactured synthetically, but to date the diamonds that have been produced in the laboratory are small, poor in quality and much too expensive to threaten the market.

Naturally none of these substitutes is as hard as diamond, and as a result the commonest method of detecting substitutes is a simple surface scratch test; this can, however, be a dangerous test, since you could scratch your real diamond using it. The GIA can perform other, less hazardous tests on your stone; I advise you to seek such expert advice before submitting your uncertain stone to possible surface damage.

2. Ruby

Next to the diamond, the ruby is probably more closely associated with legend and romance than any other precious gem. It has long been considered the prince of gems in many cultures—outranking even diamonds—and its Sanskrit term, *ratnanavaka,* means "lord of the precious stones." So highly esteemed was the gem in old Burma (origin still of the world's finest specimens) that the king of that land represented himself as the "Lord of Rubies" and claimed as his own all large stones found within the kingdom.[4]

Chemically, ruby is a form of crystallized aluminum oxide whose common name is *corundum.* The stone comes in various shades of red and pink and owes its characteristic hue to minute quantities of oxidized chromium. In the most highly valued stones, this element comprises 0.1 percent of the stone's weight—producing a deep and lustrous red known as "pigeon's blood red." Another chemical addition that often finds its way into rubies is the crystallized substance rutile. When found in its characteristic "silklike" woven pattern within the stone, it imparts to the ruby a phenomenon known as "asterism," or the appearance of an internal star, which can make even the duller-colored stones valuable.

Rubies are imitated by a great variety of other stones, including spinel, zircon, topaz, garnet and quartz. So commonly have substitutes passed as the real thing in the past that in some circles you still hear worthless local imitations being spoken of as "special" or "uncommon" types of ruby. Red garnets, for example, have been called "Cape rubies," "Montana rubies" and "Syrian rubies," while the substances known as "Bohemian" and "Brazilian" rubies are in fact nothing more than deeply colored quartz. One of the most famous "rubies" of history, the "Black Prince" ruby, which was supposedly worn in the helmet of Henry V at the battle of Agincourt and which now is part of England's crown jewels, is in fact a spinel.

Generally speaking, the finest rubies today still come from Burma, although stones of considerable beauty are also mined in other parts of Southeast Asia, as well as in Sri Lanka, Tanzania, Afghanistan and North Carolina. Knowing where a stone comes from can often be a good guide to its value, since a Burmese ruby can be worth ten or twenty times as much as a similar-sized stone from nearby Thailand. Genuine rubies can vary in price from $10,000 a carat to fifty cents a carat, depending on color and on geographical origin. Even when a ruby *is* a ruby, it may not be worth a top ruby's price. A jeweler doesn't have to sell you a fake to make a big profit: he can simply sell you a Tanzanian ruby and charge you a Burmese price.

Knowledge of geography, however, is not always an adequate guide, since fine stones do come from countries other than Burma—and since,

4 Rogers and Beard, *5000 Years of Gems and Jewelry,* p. 225.

in today's substitute-rich market, you can seldom be sure if what you are getting is actually a ruby at all. I've mentioned how much less valuable a synthetic ruby is than a natural one; a similar discrepancy in value can be observed between rubies and their various natural substitutes.

3. Sapphire

One answer to the question posed by the title of this chapter is "When it's a sapphire." For sapphire, contrary to popular belief, is not really distinct from ruby. The sparkling blue of the sapphire and the deep red of the ruby are caused by chemical ingredients in the stones—in the case of the ruby, chromium, and in the case of the sapphire, iron and titanium. Apart from these minute traces of coloring agent, ruby and sapphire are chemically identical: they are both corundum, or aluminum oxide. Like rubies, sapphires are found in a variety of hues—"cornflower blue" is the most prized, but they also come in other shades of blue, gold and even red—and, like rubies, they often display an attractive, and valuable, asterism. Probably the world's most famous sapphire is the huge (535-carat) Star of India, a striking star sapphire that is now kept in New York's American Museum of Natural History.

Like rubies, sapphires are widely imitated and are manufactured synthetically as well. Depending on their trace minerals, practically all the stones that are used to imitate the ruby form of corundum are also used to imitate sapphires. Since corundum is very hard (9 on the Mohs scale), scratch tests can often detect these substitutes, but they cannot detect synthetics. Microscopic examination, as in the case of diamonds, is more valuable to the gemologist.

By general consent, the most beautiful sapphires today are thought to come from Kashmir, Burma and Sri Lanka, in that order. The stones are mined throughout Southeast Asia and are often found along with their "cousin" stones, rubies. Tanzania, Australia and our own state of Montana are other sources of the gems. The same caveats apply here with respect to geographical identification as apply in the case of rubies.

4. Emerald

Perhaps because their characteristic green color suggests the resurgence of spring, emeralds have frequently been associated with revitalization and rebirth: in the Middle Ages the emerald was a prized healing stone and was often used as a supposed antidote to poison. Whether or not these beliefs in the stone's curative power have any basis in fact, the emerald is one of the most striking of all precious gems. Its green hue makes it an equal in beauty to the blue sapphire and the red ruby, and it is not surprising that, next to diamonds, these three stones comprise a kind of magical triad of high value. Gemologists disagree about which stones are really the most desirable, but virtually everyone agrees that the front runners are diamond, ruby, sapphire and emerald. This fact is certainly reflected in the prices sought, and paid, for the gems.

Emerald is the most highly valued variety of a quite common gemstone group, the *beryl* group. It is composed chemically of beryllium aluminum silicate, with trace elements of chromium and vanadium giving it its peculiar green color. Its hardness is less than that of corundum —7.5 to 8 on the Mohs scale—and although its brilliance is less remarkable than that of the harder gems, many people feel that this "defect" is more than made up for by its color.

Emeralds are highly prized in spite of their tiny crystalline inclusions. These inclusions have been named, collectively, *jardin,* or garden, since they suggest the presence of foliage within the verdant stone. As in the case of rubies and sapphires, they are often clues to the genuine nature of the gems: synthetic emeralds, which are common, can be made much "purer" but are substantially less valuable.

Emeralds, which were mined in Egypt in Cleopatra's time, are now found in the Soviet Union's Ural Mountains, in southern Africa, and in the Austrian Alps. The finest specimens, however, come from Colombia, and particularly from its world-famous Muzo mine. Colombia has been a repository of fine emeralds for centuries, as early Latin American history testifies. The conquistadors took vast quantities of emeralds out of the Andes Mountains during the Spanish conquest, and one of the most remarkable collections of emeralds of all time was used to adorn the famous Queen of the Andes crown; a crown made to honor the Virgin Mary in 1593, it was encrusted with 453 of the green stones by the people of a tiny Colombian town.

Emeralds are easily confused with a variety of other materials, the most common of which include tourmaline, peridot, garnet, fluorite, apatite, chrysoberyl, zircon, jade and glass. I have already noted that emerald triplets—usually two pieces of glass bonded by a green cement —are among the most common assembled stones. You should know also that many of today's supposed "natural" emeralds are actually synthetic, or "Chatham," emeralds, produced in the laboratory by a process developed in the 1930s by Carroll F. Chatham. These manufactured stones can be beautiful enough, but they are worth a fraction of what natural emeralds are worth, and for that reason extreme care must be taken when purchasing even "real" emeralds. Because the inclusions of synthetic emeralds differ from those of the natural stones, gemologists can distinguish between them—but you may not always have the benefit of their expertise.

5. *Aquamarine*

What the sapphire is to the ruby, the aquamarine is to the emerald. Aquamarine, like emerald, is simply a variety of beryl, and it has the same chemical composition as emerald, beryllium aluminum silicate. The difference between the two stones is their color: the emerald's green is supplied, as I've said, by chromium and vanadium, while the lighter, bluish green of the aquamarine comes from traces of iron. This difference in color may seem slight, but it has enormous consequences for the relative values of the two stones. In spite of its popularity, aquamarine is actually on the rather hazy border between the precious and the semiprecious stones. It is therefore not always a good investment, even if you can be assured that the stone you want is genuine.

The world's best aquamarines come from Brazil, although they are also found in California, Asia and the Urals. Since beryl is found in such a large color range, it is fairly common for aquamarine—like emerald—to be mistaken for other stones, and vice versa. The best advice I can offer you to avoid the confusing, and potentially expensive, intricacies of the beryl group is to buy only what you personally like, without considering it an investment. Investing in any colored stone is hazardous, and this is especially the case with a borderline stone like aquamarine.

6. *Opal*

Because of their play of colors and their characteristic milky appearance, opals are one of the most distinctive of precious stones. To enhance their curious characteristics, they are usually cut into rounded forms, rather than faceted: the oval and the cabochon cuts are the most popular. The stones come in a wide range of hues. In spite of the fact that the most popular variety is the whitish-greenish oval cut, this is by no means the most valuable. In fact, white opal is really the least valuable variety. Most valuable is the grayish-black or dark-green stone with red, yellow and even orange highlights that gemologists call "black opal."

True black opal, which is mined most extensively in Australia, can be an extremely valuable stone, but precisely because it is so valuable, it is frequently imitated. I have already mentioned that opal doublets are among the common assembled stones: in this kind of fake, a slice of good-quality opal is glued onto a backing of poorer opal or black glass. The amount of truly precious stone that goes into such a concoction is small, and yet—because it simulates the black opal—it can be sold for many times its actual worth. White opal is also often turned into black opal by cooking it first in a sugar solution and then immersing it in acid, which turns the sugar black. These are only two examples of how a relatively valueless stone can be turned into an ostensible "bargain." The deception, again, can be discovered by a professional gemologist, and if you think you are being offered a true black opal, it's always a good idea to check, before you buy, with a professional who has no vested interest in its sale. In addition, synthetic opals have recently been put onto the market, further increasing the buyer's risks.

7. Chrysoberyl

Chrysoberyl is a relatively unsung stone, which, if it were prized solely on the basis of its rarity, would probably be the most expensive gemstone of all. It's a crystallized form of beryllium aluminate that appears in a narrow, but exotic, range of colors from yellow to chartreuse to gold. The coloring agents here are iron, chromium and occasionally titanium. The stone is only a little softer than the corundums, standing at 8.5 on the Mohs scale. Chrysoberyl is sold not only as a plain, faceted gem but also in two particularly exotic forms; in these forms it is most highly regarded—and most widely imitated.

The first eccentric form is known as *alexandrite*, after Russia's Czar Alexander II, on whose birthday it was supposedly first discovered in the Urals. Alexandrite is the most expensive and rarest of the so-called "night and day" stones (that is, it changes color depending on whether it is sitting in natural or artificial light). In daylight it ranges from moss green to bluish green, while indoors it changes to a reddish or even an amethyst purple. This remarkable property makes the gems very attractive to some buyers, and consequently they are not infrequently faked, with the most common substitutes being synthetic corundum and synthetic spinel: both of these are offered to the unwary as "synthetic alexandrite" and in some cases as actual alexandrite. Be cautious in buying any alexandrite, especially if the price is low. In my fifty years in the business, I think I have not seen more than two or three genuine, gem-quality alexandrites.

The second eccentric form of chrysoberyl is the form that, when rounded and polished, displays the property known as "chatoyancy," or the "cat's-eye" effect. This striking effect, which is caused by the play of light against tiny fibers in the interior of the stone, appears as a thin line of light wandering mysteriously over the surface of the polished gem; for those who are attracted to the magical allure as well as the simple beauty of gems, the cat's-eye effect can be a major selling point.

Again, be on your guard. If chrysoberyl were the only gem to display chatoyancy, there would be no room for confusion, but that is not the case. Cat's-eyes are also found in a variety of lesser stones, including beryl, scapolite and tourmaline; one of the most common substitutes for chrysoberyl cat's-eye is the quite pedestrian "tiger eye," which is simply a golden or brownish dyed quartz. These occidental versions of cat's-eye may be interesting enough in their own right, but they do not merit a heavy price. True oriental cat's-eye is both extremely expensive and extremely rare.

8. Topaz

The same error of attributing a precious name to common stones is evident, only more so, in the case of precious topaz. Although it comes in a variety of shades—including pink, red and blue—topaz has usually been thought of as golden or yellow, because the golden hues it displays are delightfully and radiantly warm. This has led to much confusion. On the one hand, it has led people to misrepresent true topazes as a variety of other stones; a significant error of this type was made in the identification of a large colorless topaz in the Portuguese crown jewels as, of all things, a diamond: even today, this stone is erroneously called the Braganza Diamond.

On the other hand, the term topaz has been applied, with no justification, to a huge range of less valuable stones that just happen to have a "true" topaz color: gold, yellow or brown. This terminological confusion continues today; the term topaz is still being applied to everything from chrysoberyl to glass. The most common of these false designations is the case of the common yellow citrine quartz. Citrine has been mixed up with topaz for centuries, by both honest and unscrupulous jewelers; among its common "nicknames" have been the misleading ones "quartz topaz," "smoky topaz," and "Scotch topaz." Topaz, to make matters worse, has often been referred to as "smoky quartz."

The moral: when shopping for topaz, take every claim with a grain of salt. Do not confuse color with value. Most of the world's good topaz comes from Brazil, but the rarest variety of all, which is mined in the Urals, is a soft rose pink—not the "standard" golden yellow. If you insist on buying in this tricky market, be sure you have the advice of a disinterested expert. Most of the topazes sold today are in reality semi-precious stones.

9. Jade

Jade, like topaz, is often identified incorrectly with a single color, green. Actually, jade comes in a variety of colors, ranging from apple green to brown and from lavender blue to violet; the darker, brownish colors, used in much commercial jewelry, are found in what is called "nephrite," while the more coveted, lighter hues are usually found in what is termed "jadeite." Both nephrite and jadeite are commonly referred to as jade. In the Far East, the prejudice toward the lighter greens remains, and the Chinese, who attach a mystical significance to the stone, will pay huge sums of money for what they call "Imperial" jade.

Because it is so highly valued in the East, most of the world's finest jade—the best-quality stone comes from Burma—ends up in Hong Kong, from where it is traded throughout the Orient. Unless you are in the habit of visiting Hong Kong regularly, therefore, I advise you to steer clear of jade—unless, again, you particularly like a piece for its aesthetic, rather than investment, qualities. I have seen "jade" necklaces sold for $5,000 that were obviously made not of jade but of a look-alike green stone. The same thing goes for many of the "precious jade" carvings that are sold in our major cities for prices that are ridiculously low.

10. Pearls

Unlike the other gems I've discussed, pearls are organic in nature, being the creation of various mollusks that, in response to irritants within their shells, slowly coat the intrusive material with a calcium compound until a pearl is formed. This means that they are relatively more susceptible to destruction than inorganic gems—heat is a particular enemy of pearls—but it also means that, unlike the creations of the earth, they are still being produced today. Indeed, the market for pearls is good enough that most of the world's supply is now composed not of naturally formed specimens, but of cultured pearls and other imitations. This has serious consequences for the potential investor.

In a natural pearl, the calcium compound that forms around the irritating nucleus—it's called *nacre*—is deposited by the mollusk in concentric circles, so that if you cut open a natural pearl, you would find a cross section resembling the top diagram on page 170. Quite a different process of nacre accretion takes place in a cultured pearl. When pearls are cultured, a foreign substance (usually a piece of mother-of-pearl) is introduced into the mollusk by hand, and the nacre forms around it, but in a very different pattern. In a cultured pearl, the nacre is deposited in parallel layers, so that a typical cross section would resemble the bottom diagram on page 170.

It is very difficult to discern a natural from a cultured pearl merely by examining the outside. Although the natural variety is worth many times that of the cultured variety, there is no way of telling the difference between the two unless you can get a look at the center. This is

NATURAL AND CULTURED PEARLS

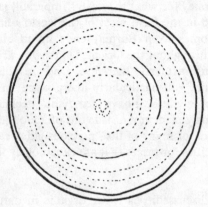

cross section of
a natural saltwater pearl

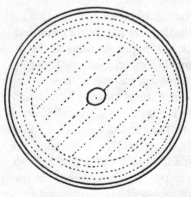

cross section of
a drilled cultured pearl

done in a number of ways, one of the most common being the use of the pearl "endoscope." In the endoscope method, the pearl bead is inspected with an instrument that combines an intense light source, a needle with a tiny mirror attached and a microscope. Looking through the microscope, the gemologist can see the inner walls of the bead reflected off the mirror, to determine whether the core is natural or cultured. (This method can be used only on drilled pearls.) Cultured pearls are also X-rayed to reveal the inner structure.

You might think that this is a lot of trouble to go to to determine the difference between two items that cannot be distinguished by the naked eye. But the value of pearls lies chiefly in the amount of nacre that is deposited relative to the size of the irritant core, and the amount of this substance is almost always greater in natural than in cultured pearls. In some cultured pearls, large glass beads are used as "starters," and the nacre is allowed to accumulate for only a very short time. To judge from the rate at which some pearl culture "farms" yank their valuable "crops" in and out of the water, you'd think they were paying the oysters by the hour. In the quickest-growing specimens, the nacre layer is so thin that you can practically see the bead beneath the surface.

The difference in price between a natural and a cultured pearl can be very great, and it increases because natural pearls are also rare. The price difference is so great that by law all nonnatural pearls must be identified as "cultured" (or "imitation" if they are not even cultured). A good-sized natural pearl can be a very good investment. But the chances of getting such a pearl for a reasonable price are slim, partly because widespread water pollution in recent years has increased the value of all pearls. If you want to get the best value for your money, be sure, before you buy, to investigate one of the testing methods I've described here. As with all the above precious gems, your watchword should be caution; again, your best advice is to stick with reliable firms. In addition, all expensive natural pearls should have GIA certificates.

"PRECIOUS" VS. "SEMIPRECIOUS"

That completes the list of the ten most popular gemstones that I would consider "precious." No doubt some of you reading this will have failed to spot your own favorite gemstone in this list, and will be asking yourselves how reliable such a list can be if it doesn't include peridot or moonstone or coral.

My response is that, although it is quite true that many other gems are often considered "precious," I have confined the above listing to those which, in my estimation, are currently most widely considered precious in the gem and jewelry markets. This is a pretty arbitrary distinction, but no more arbitrary, I assure you, than any other distinction between precious and semiprecious. One of the central things you have to remember about the gem market is that it tends to be not only extremely variable in its definitions, but capricious as well. What is today defined as precious may in ten years be defined as semiprecious, and in ten more as relatively worthless. Even if you are working only with fine, genuine specimens of gemstones, the margin for personal judgment and personal error is very large, and idiosyncratic interpretations are not uncommon.

In 1940, for example, when Frances Rogers and Alice Beard wrote their book on gems,[5] all forms of chrysoberyl were considered semiprecious gems. Today those same gems (if genuine) may bring a far higher price per carat than the emeralds these authors recognized as precious. The point is that the division between the two categories changes with time and fashion, and because of that I am half inclined to agree with Eduard Gübelin's description of the term "semiprecious" as a "linguistic monstrosity." Certainly it is a term whose connotations change from decade to decade with surprising ease.

Therefore, I could not, even if I wanted to, give you a list of precious gems that would be sure to be reliable for the remaining years of the century. The best I can do is to list those few stones—here I've called them the Top Ten—which seem to have retained their value for a reasonable period of time and which will probably continue to do so for the immediate future. There are of course numerous other gems that are lovely to look at and that you might want to purchase for adornment. Among the most popular of these "semiprecious" but still attractive gems are agate, lapis lazuli, turquoise, amethyst, garnet, coral, amber, moonstone, peridot, tourmaline and zircon. Not to mention quartz, which in spite of its somewhat unethical use as a substitute for other gems, does present some very attractive properties of its own. If these gems catch your eye, do not turn your nose up at them just because I have not discussed them as "precious" stones. Just be sure that, if you buy them, you are doing so with their aesthetic qualities in mind, not because you see them as investments. No matter how beautiful they are, they do not usually make sound investments.

Of course very much the same thing can be said of the stones I am describing as precious. Indeed, one of the major aims of this chapter has been to show you that, unless you have access to the most sophisticated

5 Ibid.

gemological equipment, you are unlikely to do well by buying any colored stones as investments. There are simply too many tricks involved in the gemstone trade, and too many common substitutes for the major stones, to make it possible for you to "invest" here without a substantial element of risk. Unless you have spent a good deal of time studying the gemstones on your own, therefore, I do not advise this field as a good one for the novice investor.

Even if you do buy well, moreover, you can still get burned in gemstones. Most gemstones you might examine will present themselves to you not as isolated, loose stones, but as elements of a piece of jewelry. For that reason, when you inspect a ruby or a sapphire, you will not be considering only the stone itself, but its setting, its cut—and the fact that it is being offered to you as part of a composite structure. The difficulty of telling real stones from frauds is only one part of the problem. Even if you know absolutely that the three opals you are looking at in that ring are in fact genuine opals, there is still a compelling reason to be wary of purchasing them as an investment, as long as they are part of the ring. Let's look into that reason now.

CHAPTER 11

MIDDLEMEN, MARKUPS AND MORALS

You will recall the story I told in the Introduction to this book about the young man who had purchased a diamond ring for $300, only to discover, when he decided to sell it, that it was worth about one sixth that amount. His problem was not that he had been sold a fake diamond or fool's gold, but that he had paid an inflated price for low-grade gold and a cheap stone. This kind of situation is far from uncommon in the jewelry business. In the last chapter, I mentioned that there are two main reasons you should steer clear of "investing" in jewelry. The first reason—the prevalence of fakes and cheap imitations—I discussed in that chapter. The second reason—the fact that even honest goods are often inflated in price—is the subject of the current chapter.

It shouldn't really come as a surprise that jewelry is commonly over-priced (in terms of the value of the materials used to make it), since, unlike an equivalent weight of pure gold, it has undergone a variety of manufacturing processes, all of which add to its selling price. As I've stressed throughout the book, when you buy anything for investment purposes, you should always strive to buy it in the simplest form possi-ble, because that is the only way you can minimize middleman charges and commissions. In the case of jewelry, this advice is very difficult to follow. All jewelry has gone through some manufacturing, and some of it has seen so many stages of manufacturing—and attendant middleman charges—that the customer ends up paying a heavy price for it even when gold and other raw materials are at rock bottom.

To explain this situation better, let's take a closer look at that ring the young man bought. Let's look at it from the time it is merely raw materials to the time it goes into his pocket, to see how many people are actually involved in setting the high price that is put on it by the retail seller. When you spend $300 for a ring that "should" cost only $50, you might think that you are the victim merely of a single, unscrupulous dealer. That is not the case; actually, you are being "victimized" by a quite natural, quite unavoidable and quite scrupulous system of accu-mulative charging. It's a system that works in any retail trade, one that I like to call the "chain of demand."

THE CHAIN OF DEMAND

Those of you who have spent any time in the service will recognize the term "chain of command." It refers to the fact that, when any decision is made, the responsibility for carrying out that decision passes in succession from the officer of highest rank to the one immediately beneath him, and so on down the line. Even though it's the lowly private who carries out most orders, ultimate responsibility for their consequences rests with the head of the command chain, the President of the United States. That is what President Truman meant when he dolefully observed, "The buck stops here."

In the jewelry (and other retail) trades, there is a similar chain in effect; only, what is passed along that chain is not responsibility for the execution of orders, but responsibility for paying the cost of a given article for sale. This is what I mean by the "chain of demand." Everyone involved in the production, manufacture and sale of a bracelet or ring has to get his or her "cut" of the ultimate selling price, but it is you, the private in the demand chain, who finally has to come up with the money to satisfy all their demands. It's an inversion of the military chain, in that the buck stops at the bottom.

Some of the young man's $300 goes directly into the pocket of the dealer (honest or dishonest) who sells him the diamond ring. But he gets only the last cut. The first cuts are taken at the source of the ring's raw materials, the gold and the uncut diamond, both of which (let's say) come out of the earth of South Africa. In South Africa, some of the people whom the young man is ultimately paying are the miners who dig the metal and stones out of the ground, the owners and other officials of the mining companies, government officials who supervise the operations, and the smelters, assayers and refiners who transform the raw gold into material that can be used in jewelry.

Up to this point, all of the charges that have accumulated in the gold and diamond would have accumulated anyway, whether they were going to be used in industrial processes, in coinage or in jewelry. Even if you buy gold in bullion form, you end up paying for the work done on it up to this point. But, from here on, the charges that begin to accumulate are part of the jewelry chain of demand, and it is these charges that account for the inflated price that the young man eventually pays.

After the gold leaves South Africa, assuming it is going to be made into his ring, it will next go through an alloying process, where it will be mixed with a percentage of base metal. Then it may go to one of the world's great ring factories, where (now in 14-karat form) it will be spun into ring-sized wire and fed into a machine that chops it off into gold bands at the rate of hundreds of rings an hour. These mass-produced gold bands will then go to a wholesale jewelry manufacturer, who will put them together with diamonds of various sizes and produce the finished rings.

The diamonds that this manufacturer uses, of course, will already have gone through their own chain of demand. After leaving South Africa, they will have traveled to Antwerp or Tel Aviv or New York, where they will have been faceted and polished by cutters, to the specific requirements of the jewelry wholesaler. Take into account in addition the various handling personnel and security forces and insurance people involved, and you will realize that, even before it leaves the wholesale jeweler, the young man's ring has already been "handled," directly or indirectly, by a considerable number of middlemen. And all of them must be paid.

Once the ring passes from the wholesaler to the retailer, it may still not have completed its chain of demand. The first retailer who receives it may not be able to sell it as quickly as he had anticipated, and he may in turn sell it, at a sacrifice price, to a dealer with a better market for it. This could happen two or three times before the young man first sees the ring—and he will therefore end up paying not one retailer but several, since all of them will expect to make a little profit on their sales. You can see that, by the time all the middlemen have been paid, the young man is going to be shelling out a great deal in fees that he would not have had to pay if he had bought a relatively "plain" item like an unset diamond or gold bullion.

Probably the largest portion of the middleman charges—not counting the retailer's cut—is in the cost of workmanship. Labor costs, especially for skilled labor, are a steep percentage of end cost in any manufactured item, and this is definitely the case when the item is a piece of fine jewelry.

To give you an idea of how crucial labor costs are in determining the end price of, for example, a gold item, let me note how labor charges are figured into the cost of one of the most common uses of gold: dental fillings. Since the gold rush of the late 1970s, I have been buying thousands of dollars' worth of gold fillings each year, and it is sobering to realize, when you weigh these unintentional "investments" in the precious metal, just how much of their cost has been a labor markup over the melt value. The average large filling—most of which, incidentally, are not 24-karat gold but are alloyed with platinum or silver—contains about $15 worth of gold at current prices. Yet to get that filling put into your teeth, you would expect to pay probably no less than a couple of hundred dollars to the dentist. What you pay that extra $185 for is the expertise and training of the professional who fills your cavity—in other words, you pay it in labor costs.

That is an extreme example of how labor charges inflate the cost of worked materials, since few laborers, no matter how skilled, take home anywhere near a dentist's hourly rate. But the principle remains the same. Whether your ring is designed and crafted by a "name" jeweler with a list of celebrity clients or by a run-of-the-mill craftsperson who churns out several rings a day, the price you pay for the ring is going to reflect, to a great degree, the time and labor put into it by the various middlemen with "hands-on" jewelry experience. No matter how little the metal is selling for per ounce, if you buy it in the form of jewelry, you will end up paying many times its spot price.

Finally—in case you are still considering buying jewelry as an "investment"—consider the heaviest link of all in the chain of demand: the retailer. The cut that he or she takes out of the selling price is so large that it makes even the previous labor costs look small by comparison.

THE FINAL—AND BIGGEST—CUT

There has been a lot of talk in the press recently about profit levels for American businesses, and about how much profit is "fair" or "ethical" in these times of economic stress. The oil companies in particular have been taken to task for achieving so-called "obscene" levels of profit, and business people have frequently been put on the defensive trying to explain and justify their successes.

As many executives have pointed out, the rate of return on investment, in spite of those "obscene" profits, has more often than not been quite low, and even those companies that achieve remarkably high rates of return still have to contend with rising overhead, rising labor costs, fluctuating markets and other aspects of the financial picture which tend to make their successes less a cause for rejoicing than they might be in more stable times. This is not the place to debate the merits of the pro-profit versus anti-profit arguments. I just want to point out that, if you wanted to pick an industry that illustrates clearly how large profits and real success are not always identical, you could do better than choose the oil companies. You could look at the jewelry industry, because in that industry the people who make the most profit of all—in terms of their cut of the chain of demand—are often the ones whose businesses are actually the weakest link in that chain. It is one of the curiosities of the jewelry trade that the retailer, who is more often than not a small, hardworking businessman, not a mogul, has to charge a quite enormous rate of "profit" just in order to survive. That is to say, it is the little guy who sells you the ring who is actually responsible for the biggest markup of all.

In the jewelry industry the *standard* markup—that is, the one generally considered fair and ethical—is 100 percent over wholesale. Retailers say that they work on a 50 percent profit margin, but what this means is that 50 percent of the selling price of their goods is their cut of the selling price: their markup, in other words, is 100 percent. The ring that Mr. Dealer sells the young man for $300 he actually bought at wholesale for $150. That is, he paid that much for it if he is an ethical dealer. If he is a bucket-shop operator or one of the fly-by-night dealers that now infest the jewelry market, he may have paid $100 or $25 for it —and still unloaded it for $300.

A 100 percent markup would hardly be considered ethical in most retail trades, but in the jewelry trade it is thought to be a necessity. That is because in this trade retailers must hold on to their inventory for a much longer time than retailers do in other trades. The turnover rate is so slow that, when they finally do sell the ring, they have to justify keeping it on the books by asking a much stiffer selling price than would otherwise have been necessary.

In a grocery store, for example, cereal boxes do not sit on the shelves for six months before someone buys them. The grocery turnover rate is swift, and as a result grocers can afford to get by on a relatively low profit margin. The jeweler, however, can easily keep a ring in stock for six or eight or twelve months, and during all that time he has not only tied up his money in the ring, but has also paid insurance charges on it and of course used some of his shelf space. It costs him money to keep the ring in stock, and he needs to make some of that money back each time he sells an item. It's a commonsense dictum in retailing that, the slower your turnover rate, the higher you have to make your markup.

In stores that have a better turnover rate, this dictum is somewhat modified. Since they do a pretty brisk trade and since their inventory is small in comparison with their sales, they can afford to survive on a somewhat reduced profit margin, and as a result you can sometimes buy jewelry at far less than the usual 100 percent markup. Some jewelers discount, in other words, because they can afford to—and even so, they make a quite healthy return on their sales.

In the age of high interest rates, this necessity to keep profit margins high has even forced some jewelers out of business. Say you are a small-time jeweler with $20,000 to invest either in more stock or in some other venture. You know that if you buy more inventory, two thirds of it may sit on your shelves for a year or more and you will realize no return on it at all. On the other hand, you can put that $20,000 into a money-market fund (where it will give you a very good return), liquidate your stock gradually and begin to make money off your money, rather than off your beautiful but immovable stones. Many small dealers have done just that.

What I'm saying here applies to the everyday, honest Joe who runs the local retail shop and lives a more or less comfortable existence based on the 50 percent profit margin that is conventional in the industry. In certain cases, however, that profit margin is stretched even further—beyond the bounds of honest dealing—and in these cases the retail cut can push the selling price up to ridiculous heights.

One of these cases is that of the dealer who sells a piece of jewelry "on memorandum" and yet fails to inform the buyer of the fact. This happens a lot today, as we move through the wake of the 1970s investment-diamond explosion and the industry tries to adjust its prices to a more reasonable level.

When a dealer sells you a ring that is on memorandum, he is collecting two fees at once—although you may not know it. Say you want to buy a one-carat diamond, but your local dealer does not have the type you want in stock. If he is determined to make a sale, what he may do is to stall you a couple of days and secure one on memorandum from a wholesaler. "I have that kind of stone in my other vault," he might say. "Can you come back Wednesday?" Then he will ask his wholesaler to supply the kind of stone you want; he will not have to pay for it yet, since it is being given to him on the understanding that he will "buy" it only after he "sells" it to you. This is what is meant by selling on memorandum.

The trouble in the system arises when the stone has been sitting in the wholesaler's stock for two or three years because he bought it at an old, inflated price and has not been able to unload it. To make up for the drop in market prices since he bought the stone, he lets the retailer sell it to you at the old, inflated price—plus the retailer's own markup. You end up paying the standard 100 percent markup on a price that is already too high by current standards—and both the wholesaler and the retailer profit from your ignorance.

Even when you don't buy in the dark like this, you can still be the victim of erratic markup policies. I noted in the last chapter how variable are the prices for gems, and this variability, even among honest dealers, can lead to real trouble for the buyer. A ruby, as I've pointed out, can be worth anything from 50 cents a carat to $10,000 a carat, depending on where it comes from, what quality it is, and so on. If you don't know the difference between the two kinds of stones, you may end up spending the quality-stone rate for a stone that should be only costume jewelry. And if you confront the dealer with this afterward, you will not have a leg to stand on. There are no standards in the colored-stone industry, remember—so all he has to say is that he sold you a "real ruby," as he promised.

The prevalence of memorandum selling and of the great variance in jewelry values are only two of the many elements that bedevil the jewelry industry and make it a morass of confusion even for many people inside the industry. How much more confusing it can be for someone whose only notion of jewelry comes from his attraction to Aunt Bessie's "real ruby" ring that has lain in the attic for twenty years!

Because there are no set standards to judge gems and because of the number of middlemen involved, the abundance of imitations and the prevailing high-markup system, I do not in general advise anyone interested in investment to put his or her trust in jewelry. There are exceptions, of course: cases in which buying an old or particularly interesting article of jewelry will prove, in the long run, to have been a good investment. Buying antique jewelry in particular can be an especially lucrative business. But it is a specialty business, like investing in Georgian silver or rare stamps, and unless you have a firm background in antiques in general and jewelry in particular, I advise you to keep away from that bona fide Louis XIV sapphire brooch: it may well turn out to have been made in Brooklyn, circa 1982.

TO HAVE AND TO HOLD

This is not to say that buying jewelry is in itself a bad idea. On the contrary, there are many compelling reasons to purchase fine jewelry: it is beautiful, it is useful as an adornment, it brings pleasure, it can serve as a lifelong memento, and so on. While I would never advise anyone to purchase a diamond bracelet as a hedge against inflation, this is very different from saying, "Don't buy jewelry at all." I have been dealing with jewelry for over fifty years, and I would be the last to deny that buying it can be a delightful and satisfying experience. I am fully in accord with De Beers when they say that there is nothing quite like a diamond to enhance remembrance of a particular event, be it an anniversary, a graduation or a birth. For the other gemstones too, I have a very high regard.

All I am saying is that, when you set out to purchase an article of jewelry, you should get your expectations straight. Do not imagine that having a diamond bracelet in your safety-deposit box is going to protect you against the ravages of inflation ten years from now. Because of the reasons I've pointed out in this and the previous chapter, the chances are very good that, when you go to sell your "investment," you will be able to realize on it only a fraction of what you paid for it—even considering inflation. To break even on a piece of jewelry these days, you would have to get it at true wholesale, and hold on to it for a decade—and such "bargains," as I've noted, generally exist only in the buyer's imagination.

But if a piece of jewelry attracts you—if you think it would be just the thing to cement a burgeoning relationship or to mark the anniversary of an old one—by all means "invest" in it. Buying a diamond bracelet for your spouse, I suppose, can be a kind of special investment in itself: an investment in the affection two people hold for each other. It's not accidental that jewelry—especially fine diamond jewelry—has been used for many centuries to signify the importance of personal milestones. It has always provided, and it will continue to provide, a particularly striking visual symbol of what can only be felt, not seen. For this reason, I heartily approve of buying good jewelry of any kind. As long as a piece will bring someone pleasure, it's beside the point to worry about how many middlemen you are keeping in caviar when you write your jeweler a check.

But when you buy, buy with care. Just because that brooch is bound to delight your spouse, there is no reason to pay $400 a carat for it if it's glass. Before you shop, recall the common imitations of favorite gemstones. Be sure to deal only with people whose reputation you can verify. And insist on a buy-back guarantee. Even if you are buying only for the delight of owning a beautiful article, there is no point in paying more than you must.

Remember especially that, in the jewelry business, unlike the "plain" metals or diamonds business, there is very little control over what a dealer can say or do to get you to buy his or her products. The standards in this business, as I've noted several times, are by no means firmly established, and as a result one person's "star sapphire" can easily be another one's squandered paycheck. When you buy a one-ounce wafer of .999 fine gold from a recognized refiner, you know exactly what you are getting and can verify the going rate for such a purchase in any daily newspaper. No such certainty exists in the jewelry market: in this market, the terminology itself is a rat's nest of idiosyncracy and confusion.

The jewelry industry itself has gradually come to recognize that the miasma of differing terms and the lack of industry standards hurt dealers as much as the public—and it has recently decided that, in everyone's best interests, something must be done about this situation. The suggestion for imposing fairly regular standards on the jewelry industry came originally from the Jewelers Vigilance Committee, an organization that polices, and insists on fair practices from, its members. Their reforms, if adopted, will not make jewelry "investment" any more a sure thing than it is now, but they should remove some of the confusion.

A CHANGING INDUSTRY?

As far back as 1957, the American jewelry industry recognized that many of its trade practices and definitions were open to discussion, and as a result it set about clarifying its own basic working procedures by issuing a set of Trade Practice Rules. These rules remained in effect, and were observed with as much regularity as you could expect, into the 1970s, at which time consumer pressure on the Federal Trade Commission, which oversees the jewelry industry, led to a government review. That review, like most government reviews, took several years to complete, and between the time it began and the time the FTC issued its initial ruling, in October of 1978, the industry began its own review. In the words of William Preston, who coordinated the Jewelers Vigilance Committee's work on reviewing the rules, the jewelers alliance itself was "off and running before the ax fell." Working with considerably greater speed than the FTC, the JVC came up with a revised version of the industry guidelines in 1980—only two years after the government ruling.

The JVC submitted its recommendations for revision of the industry guidelines to the FTC in January of 1981, thus throwing the ball into the government's court. Confronted with the JVC initiative, the government agency had to decide whether it would accept the recommendations as written, accept them with changes or reject them completely and keep its own working guidelines. To date, the FTC has not yet ruled on the matter, and given the commission's performance record for responding to industry initiatives, it will probably be some time before the business is finally settled.

In the meantime, what is happening to the industry? Is it more or less confused in its definitions than it was before the FTC review?

It's probably about the same, at least as far as industry definitions have any bearing on what might interest a small investor or purchaser of jewelry. And (here is the funny part) this will probably still be the case even *after* the FTC makes its final ruling. The reason is that most of the definitions being debated are fairly sticky, technical ones that have only a passing interest for the purchaser of fine jewelry.

Not that they are irrelevant. In this book, you have already encountered many of the terms being debated, and the decisions that the government makes on them will therefore have an effect on anyone who buys jewelry. The terms "gold-plated" and "sterling," for example, are both under discussion, as are the terms "cultured pearl" and "flawless" and even "gemstone." Naturally the way these terms are officially defined will have a bearing on what kind of labeling is going to be considered permissible in the industry, and this in turn will have a bearing on what kinds of borderline practices—such as the use of the term "solid gold" to describe gold that is a solid alloy of 14-karat gold—will be acceptable in the future.

But, in a sense, whatever the FTC decides, the basic difficulties of the industry will remain. Dealers of essentially good faith will continue to adhere, as they have in the past, to generally accepted standards of ethical behavior, and if the FTC ruling makes it more difficult for them to use misleading terms like "solid gold," that will clearly be to the customer's advantage. But what about the less-than-scrupulous dealer? What about the guy who has never observed any of the industry guidelines in the past? Is it at all likely that he will observe more stringent guidelines in the future?

Obviously the answer is no, and so you the buyer must still be on your guard when dealing in a field that is so susceptible to misleading practices. The JVC took seventy-seven pages of close type to tell the FTC what it felt would be fair labeling practices. But since certain dealers are not going to abide by those practices no matter what anyone says, you have to do one of two things. Either you have to deal only with known quantities (the dealer who has been at the same address for twenty years) or you have to be suspicious of everyone.

This may sound harsh, but in a field that involves so many good opportunities for a dealer to make a killing off ignorance, it is only common sense. Whether or not the jewelry industry changes as a result of the JVC-proposed reforms, one thing will not change: the presence, in the midst of the tightest controls, of a few slippery fish who get through the regulatory net.

I am often asked whether or not I think that the jewelry business is essentially an ethical business. In other words, what proportion of slippery fish are there swimming after your money in comparison to the honest dealers? I can answer that only by saying that the presence of even one dishonest dealer makes the market very different from what it would be if all people told the truth and dealt fairly with the public. If they were all models of probity and justice, of course, we wouldn't need any regulations at all.

Ten years ago, I would have said that the great majority of people in the jewelry business are honest, straightforward tradesmen. Today I'm not so sure. Because of the diamond and gold explosions of the 1970s, many people have entered the industry who were selling soap or shoe-laces or automobile parts a decade ago and have become purveyors of bracelets and rings simply because they saw a quick buck to be made and hopped after it. Probably the majority of the jewelers you will confront are pretty honest, but then, a majority is only 51 percent, and sorting them out from the huge numbers of fly-by-nighters can be a hazardous and unrewarding task.

That is why I must reiterate once again something that I have noted many times in the course of this book: when shopping for an "invest-ment," always know whom you are dealing with, and always be sure that you have a sound, written guarantee in case you are disappointed with your purchase once you get it home. If you buy a ring without these two basic assurances, no power on earth—not even the FTC—can bail you out of trouble.

This is what I have been saying not only about jewelry, but about purchasing precious metals and stones as well, and it is an appropriate note on which to end this book. There is no such thing as too much caution in the fields of gold, silver and diamonds. Even when buying and selling "plain," unadorned metals, you should keep this principle in mind—and you should keep it doubly in mind when your purchases are manufactured for adornment.

There are fortunes yet to be made in the exciting world of gold, silver and diamonds, but your best single rule of thumb, when entering that world, is to acquire a suspicious nature. Being on your guard for the many things that can go wrong in this exotic type of investment is your best protection against being caught in the middle when the worst that can happen does happen. It is also your best assurance that, when you decide to buy or sell, you will be doing so with the greatest chance of success.

And success, after all, is what buying and selling gold, silver and diamonds is all about. Reading the opportunities for success with a judicious, well-informed mind is what separates the young man with the nearly worthless diamond ring from the person of no greater means who has managed to parlay his small purchase into something that really will increase in value over the years. It is what can make you, if you follow the guidelines of this book carefully, one of that growing number of people for whom precious metals and stones are not only a source of aesthetic delight, but a means to sound financial growth as well.

CONCLUSION

GUIDELINES FOR THE SMART INVESTOR

In this book, I have tried to present to you the basic information you need to enter the fascinating and potentially lucrative world of investing in gold, silver and diamonds. It is my hope that, by reading it, you will have come to a sound understanding of how these precious commodities are commonly bought and sold, and gained an appreciation of some of the intricacies of the market. As many new investors have discovered in recent years, trading in gold, silver and diamonds can be an extremely exciting pastime, with the potential for providing a solid buffer against inflation, not to mention considerable aesthetic delight.

But, as I've stressed repeatedly, there are also major pitfalls in this specialized investment field—as some of those new investors have found out to their chagrin. If you have read the book carefully, you will already have gained some insight into the darker side of the metals and diamonds investment promise—and learned how to spot some of the more common tricks of this glamorous trade. I'd like to end the book by reiterating the major caveats you should keep in mind as you shop around with a few hundred or a few thousand dollars in your pocket and your eye on a "surefire" thing.

The first thing to remember, of course, is that there are no "surefire" things in the gold, silver or diamond market. I never tell any of my customers that a given purchase will be "certain" to increase at such-and-such a rate over the next five years, and anyone who gives you this kind of assurance is fooling himself, you or both. What I do give them, and what I can give you here by way of conclusion, is a few fundamental purchasing principles.

You can think of these principles as a kind of ten commandments of playing the precious-investments game. I can't guarantee that, if you follow them, you will be rivaling the Hunts by next month. But I can guarantee that, if you ignore them, you will almost certainly come out badly.

1. Do Your Homework

Read as much as possible about your potential investment before you ever walk into a shop. Go over the parts of this book that apply to your particular interest and study them in detail. Check the Bibliography, at the end of the book, for further information, and talk to as many people in the field—starting with your banker, broker or investment counselor —as you can before actually committing any money. Watch the market, and plan to buy—and sell—at the most advantageous times, not just when the "mood" hits you. Remember that you are not playing the ponies, but trying to make a judicious decision about an inflation-fighting investment. The more you know about gold or silver or diamonds before you shop, the better that decision will be.

2. Shop Around

No two dealers have precisely the same schedule of rates and fees, so it is always to your advantage to compare prices before you invest. This applies whether you are buying or selling. To get the best price in either case, you have to try several places. Uncle Joe, down the block, may be a perfectly honest fellow, but he is not going to be your best bet if his commissions are out of line. Remember that, legally, a dealer can charge any commission he wants; since his fee has no bearing in most cases on the intrinsic value of your purchase, get several opinions on the worth of the item that interests you before you make a decision. The bulk of your buying price should go toward the intrinsic value of your purchase, not toward keeping a dealer in Cadillacs.

3. Buy from a Reputable Dealer

Once you have narrowed your potential dealers down to those with reasonable fees, check their reputations with the Better Business Bureau, the state attorney general's office and/or the Federal Trade Commission. Avoid firms that have been in business only a short while, since you cannot know whether or not they will turn out to be fly-by-nights, interested only in taking your money and running. Many new businesses, of course, are perfectly honest, but you will still be taking the safer course if you stick with people who have been around for a long time and are known as stable members of the community.

4. Buy Close to Spot

The daily spot prices of gold and silver are published in most newspapers every day. When shopping for these metals, try to purchase them at a price as close as possible to the per-ounce spot price for that day.

Always check the spot on the day you are going to buy, and estimate before you walk into a bank or store how much you should expect to pay for a given item or quantity of the metal. Figure in dealers' fees, and favor the dealer whose per-ounce price is closest to the day's fixed rate. Use the same pretransaction calculations when you are about to sell. You will never get the full day's spot price when you sell, but aim for getting as close to it as you can.

5. Buy Pure and Plain

Remember that the more work that goes into an article, the more you will be paying in middleman and markup charges. That is why jewelry is generally not a good investment and why the best buys—in terms of investment, rather than aesthetic, qualities—are the simplest and purest forms of the metal or stone. In gold and silver, aim for .999 fineness and favor the plain, unworked bars or wafers. In diamonds, aim for the best color and clarity, and avoid fancy settings and odd cuts. Remember that buying a half ounce of pure gold plus a single one-carat brilliant diamond will always cost you a fraction of the price that you would pay for these two items if they were combined into a bracelet or a ring.

6. Get a Guarantee

Insist on a written guarantee of authenticity whenever you buy precious metals or stones. In the case of diamonds, this would be a Gemological Institute of America certificate, plus the dealer's own guarantee that he will buy back the stone within a specified period of time if you are dissatisfied with it. In the case of precious metals, get the dealer's guarantee, and be sure it includes a buy-back policy. Having a buy-back policy will enable you to get your purchase independently appraised after you buy and allow you to take it back for a refund if the appraisal turns up something the dealer "forgot" to mention. And be sure that the buy-back guarantee is favorable to you in terms of "bid" and "ask" prices: there is no point in having such a policy if the dealer agrees only to buy back your purchase at half the price you paid for it.

7. Invest Only Risk Capital

I am continually asked by novice gold and silver buyers how much they should put into an initial investment. The only reasonable rule of thumb here is to limit your investments to "risk capital"; that is, to invest only what you can afford to lose should the investment not work out. This should be a basic principle of speculation as well as investment, although it is not observed by all speculators. Avoid the speculators' "go for broke" attitude, because "broke" may be exactly what you get if you overextend yourself. Remember that "hedging" against inflation is just that: a buffer against future money troubles. It is not an alternate savings account, and should never be considered as safe a way of protecting your money as a bank account or a money-market fund. There are indeed fortunes to be made in the gold, silver and diamond markets—but there are no guarantees.

8. Be Patient

Speculators, expecting a quick kill, often dash in and out of the precious-metals and -stones markets as if they are using a revolving door—and many of them get caught in that door. Avoid this kind of "quick in, quick out" approach. Be prepared to hold on to your investments for a reasonable period of time: at least two or three years, and longer if at all possible. Do not be unduly alarmed by the daily fluctuations of the market, because in the long run—assuming wise purchasing practice—the returns on precious metals and stones have historically proved quite sound. Think of the money you put into these commodities as a seed that you plant in the ground. To have that seed grow into a fruit-bearing plant, you have to allow it time to mature.

9. Insure Yourself

Even before you take possession of your stones or metals (assuming you wish to take possession), be sure they are properly insured. Rent a safety-deposit box, or if you keep them in a home safe, be sure its contents are covered on your homeowner's policy. If you choose not to take possession, check with the dealer or bank to be certain your ownings are insured through them, and get a certificate indicating exactly what you own and where it is. Insurance charges for such valuables are generally so nominal that it is foolhardy not to pay them.

10. Be Wary

This should be the cardinal rule for all trading in gold, silver and diamonds. Remember that even honest dealers have a vested interest in profit and are not obliged to give you a good deal. Do not be bowled over by "bargains." Search for the best deal you can find, but expect to pay a fair, going rate for anything you buy. The buy that is "too good to be true" may turn out to be just that.

Those are your ten commandments. I have been involved in buying and selling precious metals and stones for over fifty years, so these guidelines are the fruit of extensive, and often hard-won, experience. It is my hope that they will help you become a smarter, more cautious and more successful participant in this sometimes confusing—but always fascinating—field.

BIBLIOGRAPHY

General

BROWNE, HARRY. *New Profits from the Monetary Crisis.* New York: Warner Books, 1978.

CARABINI, LOUIS, ed. *Everything You Need to Know Now About Gold and Silver.* Westport, Conn.: Arlington House, 1974.

CASEY, DOUGLAS R. *Crisis Investing.* New York: Pocket Books, 1980.

HUDGEONS, MARC. *The Official Investors Guide to Buying and Selling Gold, Silver and Diamonds.* Orlando, Fla.: House of Collectibles, 1981.

Gold

CAVELTI, PETER C. *How to Invest in Gold.* Chicago: Follett, 1979.

COHEN, DANIEL. *Gold: The Fascinating Story of the Noble Metal Through the Ages.* New York: M. Evans, 1976.

GREEN, TIMOTHY. *How to Buy Gold.* New York: Walker, 1975.

———. *The World of Gold Today.* New York: Walker, 1973.

HOPPE, DONALD. *How to Invest in Gold Coins.* Westport, Conn.: Arlington House, 1973.

International Monetary Market. *Understanding Trading in Gold Futures.* Chicago Mercantile Exchange Public Information and Marketing Department, 1978.

Investors Guide: Gold Bullion and Coins. What's It Worth Price Guides. New York: Dell Books, 1982.

ROSEN, LAWRENCE. *When and How to Profit from Buying and Selling Gold.* Homewood, Ill.: Dow Jones, 1975.

SINCLAIR, JAMES, and HARRY SCHULTZ. *How the Experts Buy and Sell Gold Bullion, Gold Stocks, and Gold Coins.* Westport, Conn.: Arlington House, 1975.

Silver

JASTRAM, ROY. *Silver: The Restless Metal.* New York: John Wiley, 1981.

PICK, FRANZ. *Silver: How and Where to Buy and Hold It.* New York: Pick Publishing, 1979.

SARNOFF, PAUL. *Silver Bulls: The Great Silver Boom and Bust.* Westport, Conn.: Arlington House, 1980.

WHITE, BENJAMIN. *Silver: Its History and Romance.* (1920; repr. Gale, 1971).

WYLER, SEYMOUR B. *The Book of Old Silver.* New York: Crown, 1937; repr. 1971.

Diamonds

EPSTEIN, EDWARD JAY. "Have You Ever Tried to Sell a Diamond? *Atlantic Monthly,* February 1982.

GAAL, ROBERT, ed. *The Diamond Dictionary,* 2nd ed. Santa Monica, Calif.: Gemological Institute of America, 1977.

GREEN, TIMOTHY. *The World of Diamonds.* New York: Morrow, 1981.

LEGRAND, JACQUES, ed. *Diamonds: Myth, Magic, and Reality.* New York: Crown, 1980.

SCHUMACH, MURRAY. *The Diamond People.* New York: Norton, 1981.

Jewelry

GÜBELIN, EDUARD. *The Color Treasury of Gemstones.* New York: Thomas Y. Crowell, 1975.

HURLBUT, CORNELIUS, and GEORGE SWITZER. *Gemology.* New York: John Wiley, 1979.

Jewelers Vigilance Committee. Recommendations and Explanations for Revision of "Guides for the Jewelry Industry." Presented to the Federal Trade Commission, January 8, 1981.

LIDDICOAT, RICHARD T. JR. *Handbook of Gem Identification,* 8th ed. Santa Monica, Calif.: Gemological Institute of America, 1969.

ROGERS, FRANCES, and ALICE BEARD. *5000 Years of Gems and Jewelry.* Philadelphia, Pa.: Stokes, 1940.

INDEX